The Story of an Adult Survivor
of Childhood Sexual Abuse
and His Journey to Wholeness

I'M STILL HERE

by the Grace of God

PASTOR RUSS NEBHUT

emerge
publishing
TULSA, OKLAHOMA

24 23 22 21 20 19 9 8 7 6 5 4 3 2 1

I'M STILL HERE—BY THE GRACE OF GOD
The Story of an Adult Survivor of Childhood Sexual Abuse

Disclaimer: The story, experiences, and words in this book are the author's alone and do not necessarily reflect those of Emerge Publishing. This is a personal biography of the author's life and the challenges he faced. It is intended to help others who have experienced similar issues, and also as a resource to those who counsel with victims of abuse. For this reason, the book is being published ***as told by the author***.

Published by:
Emerge Publishing, LLC
9521 Riverside Parkway, Suite 243 Tulsa, OK 74137
Phone: 888.407.4447 www.EmergePublishing.com

Library of Congress Cataloging-in-Publication Data:

ISBN: 978-1949758-40-5 Paperback
ISBN: 978-1949758-41-2 E-book

BISAC:
FAM001010 FAMILY & RELATIONSHIPS / Abuse / Child Abuse
REL050000 RELIGION / Christian Ministry / Counseling & Recovery
SEL001000 SELF-HELP / Abuse

Endorsements

I'm Still Here is a compelling read. Russ takes you through his own very intense personal journey from horror and heartache to health and healing. I highly recommend this for anyone who has experienced sexual abuse or those who work with and know survivors. Bravo Russ!

Robert Hart,
Professional Counselor and Director of
Living Hope Christian Counseling Service

Pastor Russ Nebhut candidly relives his childhood surviving as a sexual assault victim. Abused boys may never tell, ***I'm Still Here*** will allow males who were victimized at any age to know they are not alone. After his childhood was taken by his abuser, his life demonstrates that it is never too late to tell, and it is never too late to heal. Nebhut's life story provides hope, showing victims' can do more than survive, they can thrive.

Susan H. Oliva,
Executive Director
Advocacy Center for the Children of El Paso

Russ Nebhut's very existence today is a black-eye to Satan. ***I'm Still Here*** is a primer to educate us of Satan's modus operandi. Russ' story begins with vile betrayal by a guardian authority figure. Russ exposes the strategy of Satan himself to stalk and target vulnerable and innocent children. He uncovers the grooming and unspeakable abuse of which wicked people would like everyone to be ignorant. It is more heart-breaking than the story of Joseph in the book of Genesis. But the same Yahweh that rescued and brought a blessed life to Joseph is still rescuing people today. Russ Nebhut is irrefutable evidence. Russ can say I have been where you are to the abused and betrayed. He can also lead the hurting out of a life of pain and torment to a life of peace, wholeness and joy.

I'm Still Here is a handbook on how Jesus can heal and bless through Forgiveness.

Richard Bartlett MD

Broken Things

by Matthew West

If grace was a kingdom
I stopped at the gate
Thinking I don't deserve to pass through
after all the mistakes that I've made

Oh but I heard a whisper
As Heaven bent down
Said, "Child, don't you know that
the first will be last and the last get a crown"

Now I'm just a beggar in the presence of a King
I wish I could bring so much more
But if it's true You use broken things
Then here I am Lord, I'm all Yours

The pages of history they tell me it's true
That it's never the perfect; it's always the ones with the scars that You use

It's the rebels and the prodigals; it's the humble and the weak
All the misfit heroes You chose
Tell me there's hope for sinners like me

Now I'm just a beggar in the presence of a King
I wish I could bring so much more

But if it's true You use broken things
Then here I am Lord, I'm all Yours
Grace is a kingdom
With gates open wide
There's a seat at the table just waiting for you
So, come on inside

Used with Permission

Contents

Foreword

by Stephanie Nebhut

My name is Stephanie. I am Russell Nebhut's wife and he is the love of my life. I have walked this road with Russ for the last nine years and I am continually amazed at the growth and healing that I see daily.

Abuse is like a cancer. The hurt goes down so much farther than just surface deep. There is so much emotional control on the part of the abuser that it affects every part of the victim's life and raises its ugly head differently in every season of life. This book is so important, especially for male survivors, because there has traditionally been a stigma attached to this facet of abuse. Men in general have a harder time admitting to being a victim of abuse because of macho man stereotypes. I have witnessed the struggle that my husband has had in reconciling the fact that it was a small child that was abused rather than an adult man. I have also witnessed the defining and beautiful moments in people's lives when they have heard his story, and it frees them to tell their own.

It has freed people to tell their own stories. This is so important, because by telling our stories-we expose layer upon layer to the light.

The darkness has power, if we allow it. The more we discuss this subject, the more safe spaces we will have for people to reveal their hurt and the more equipped we will be to love and walk with them.

Stephanie Nebhut

Dedication

As I sit to write this dedication near the end of many years of both work and personal growth, I have only one person on my heart. It is very true that for an abused person to open up and tell one person about their abuse takes a great amount of courage. It is just as true that the person being told is just as courageous. You will hear throughout the pages of this story of a lonely dirt road and two people sitting together in a car. You will hear of fear and tears and the reality of love, acceptance, and affirmation. Over the many roads I have taken in my life, it can say with absolute assurance the day I traveled that particular road was the day which saved my life.

I desire to be very clear in what I am about to say! I fully affirm God's love, grace, and forgiveness for me in Jesus Christ. He is my Savior and for His love I am eternally grateful. But on that lonely dirt road, sitting with the woman who would later become my wife, I was saved. I was saved primarily from myself and the horror of years of abuse which had crippled my life and held me in bondage. I was saved on that day because for the first time I personally experienced unconditional love and acceptance, even in all my brokenness. I had understood for years that God was loving and gracious. I knew in my head what unconditional love was all about! I had simply never experienced it in a tangible way in my life.

There on that dusty road I did experience unconditional love! It came from a woman whom I was fearful of hurting. It came from a saint of God sent to me to save me by helping me understand I was indeed lovable. The fact that she loved me when I did not love myself and when I doubted God's love, opened the way for me to truly experience the love of God in Christ and it set me on the long journey of healing and wholeness.

It is with a humble heart of gratitude which words can never fully express that I dedicate this book to my wife Stephanie. There is nothing I desire more than to love her fully and to celebrate the blessing she is in my life every day.

May all who read this book be blessed! May you also understand that God is ready and willing to use you as His servant to speak words of love and acceptance to someone who is hurting and lost. May you become someone's "Stephanie" who can open the way for God's love to touch and heal a hurting heart.

Introduction

First, I want to say thank you for picking up this book. I will tell you up front that this is not an easy story to read and it most certainly was not an easy one to write. As a man and an adult survivor of childhood sexual abuse, I have faced the fear of having my masculinity called into question. I feared losing the people I loved because I thought knowing my story would cause them to view me differently and thus they would reject me. But instead of suffering loss through sharing my story, I have experienced more freedom and love than I ever imagined possible.

Sexual abuse, once inflicted upon a child, causes the heart of the one abused to call into question everything they once believed about themselves and others. As a victim grows and matures, the normal emotional transitions people experience as they progress through their teen and young adult years are stilted. They see the world as it is. They see other people moving forward in their lives, and all the time the abuse survivor is emotionally standing still. The development of self-loathing or self-hatred begins to grow and take root in the heart. The seeds were planted when the abuse took place, simmered until normal growth and maturity caused what had been simmering to come forth in full bloom. Often in the midst of times of celebration or even great success, these feelings of worthlessness rear up and rob the adult survivor of any real joy. There is a sense that I deserve nothing good in my life. For some, this results in self-sabotage. Others are better able to hide the pain which is their constant companion.

All of this and so much more was my personal experience as an adult survivor. For more than thirty years I hid my abuse. The resulting havoc which was reaped affected many more lives than just myself as the one who carried the pain. A failed marriage, workaholism, emotional distance from family and friends, all wrapped up in the reality that not even God could love and want a person like me. Such is the harvest of the seeds sown in those dark hours of abuse.

This book is intended to be an honest and extremely true account of the abuse experienced in the life of a boy from age ten to sixteen. While addressing the actual abuse and the circumstances around those years, it addresses much more. This book spans the thirty plus years following the abuse and then the journey toward healing which began on a lonely dirt road when a man feared losing the person he loved more than life itself.

You will read of hurt. You will hear of those who loved this little boy and those who failed in their relationship with him. Through it all, you will see God is present and working even in the midst of the times of pain and heartache, to bring something good out of such unspeakable evil.

The years of abuse were uniquely mine and the journey toward healing is also unique to me. But if there is one thing I have learned as I have shared my story and stood alongside others whose hearts were hurting from years of abuse, it is that while each story is unique, all our stories are in reality the same. We are all individuals who were created to be loved. When love is warped by abuse the resulting pain and how this pain is lived out in so many lives is very similar. It is my prayer that my experiences and the journey I have been traveling for the last ten years will enable me to walk with you on your journey toward healing. You are not alone in the suffering you have experienced. I stand with you. We all stand with you. We are adult survivors of childhood sexual abuse and we are *still here*!

Chapter One

An Innocent Beginning

I grew up watching the Andy Griffin Show. The image of Sheriff Taylor and Opie walking down the dirt road carrying their fishing poles was intensified in my life by the family who lived across the street. The family consisted of a dad, a mom, one daughter and one son. I would watch them go on family outings or the dad and son play ball in the yard. Sometimes I would be able to join in, but even when I did, I was always the outsider. I didn't have a dad. In fact, it was just my mom and me. I had a sister, but she was much older than I, so she was gone when I was still a little boy. Mom worked nights and slept in the daytime, leaving me to roam the streets and play with friends with very little supervision. It's not as bad as it sounds. The worst things we did would be considered harmless by today's standards. We would spend hours roaming the local creek and playing war games through the neighborhood. Every back yard was ours since we would jump all the fences. In the evenings, mom would get up, fix dinner and then take me across town to spend the night at my aunt's house. She would pick me up at 7:30am, take me home and I would get ready and head off to school which was only a five-block walk from the house. This was my life and it was fairly normal as I recall.

8 years old Tee-Ball

6th Grade Basketball

6th Grade Football

When school was out for the summer, I would spend time at my grandmother's home. She lived three hours away in Gainesville, a small town on the Texas and Oklahoma border. My grandmother, my mother's mother, was a feisty little woman who managed the diner at a truck stop. I say she was feisty, and while this is true, she also understood the hard realities of life. She was married when she was very young.

My grandmother was all of four-foot-eight inches tall. She was so tiny that her nickname was "Cricket". Ironically, Cricket married a man who was every bit of six-foot-five inches tall. The picture of their wedding day looks rather strange. My grandmother looks like a little girl sitting in a field leaning up against a giant of a man. Together they had five children—two boys and three girls. I have been able to learn from some relatives just what kind of a man he truly was. Henry Briggs was a very abusive man. He would beat my grandmother when he was drunk and when he was sober. He was violent in every way. As their children got older, he began to beat them as well. When the boys were old enough to understand what was happening to their mother, they would try to stop him, which resulted in an extra severe beating for them. All five kids grew up living in fear and the absence of any physical affection from their father.

Henry and Carrie (Cricket) Briggs
Wedding Day Picture

Looking back, I now realize this played greatly into my own relationship with my mother. Having grown up in this type of setting, she was not one to express any affectionate emotion toward others. I can remember my grandmother giving me hugs and I remember sitting on her lap as a small boy, but I have no memories of this from my mother. She was emotionally distant. Now please understand, my mother was a very good provider, but she was unable to be emotionally close. I have no doubt this contributed to her two failed marriages. Because of my closeness with my grandmother, I can look back on my early childhood with some fond memories.

When I was very little, my grandmother would take me to work with her and to keep me busy, she gave me a job. I was the official "fly killer" of the diner. The turquoise green vinyl booths were each placed against large windows which looked out onto the interstate. I went from booth to booth with my flyswatter in

My Grandmother and her children

hand, killing each and every fly which entered the restaurant. When my job was done, I would help collect dirty dishes and take them to the kitchen. I was always rewarded with a piece of pie and a shiny new quarter for my long day of work. I also learned an important lesson on customer service while working with my grandmother. I was chasing flies around the diner one day and one was very elusive. It flew to a window next to a booth which was occupied by some men eating lunch. They were all too ready and willing to oblige me when I asked them to vacate the booth so I could climb over to the window and kill that pesky fly I had been chasing. What was funny to them was no laughing matter to my grandmother. I can't remember any other time in my life when my grandmother gave me a whipping. It was a whipping I would never forget.

It was during these summers that I was made to feel special. Not only by my grandmother who was herself very special and a significant influence in my life, but by her brother, my great-uncle Jim. He was a retired oilfield worker who owned a ranch even though he lived in town. Each day, he would drive his old truck out into the country to check on his cows and to do whatever else would take most of the day to keep him out of the house. From time to time, he would ask my grandmother if I could go with him to the farm. What a great day it would be. I would sit in his lap and drive the old blacktop roads. I was not able to reach the pedals, but I could steer and I felt like a grownup. Other times he would let me ride in the bed of the truck. I would sit on the side of the bed, holding onto the headache rack, and hang over the side and talk to him in the driver's side window. (They would put a man under the jail for allowing a kid to do this today.) And then, there were the spiders! Tarantulas to be exact. Big, black, hairy tarantulas would be walking all over the road. It was a game for Uncle Jim to try to run over them. The only problem is that when a tarantula gets scared, it jumps. These were big spiders and therefore they could jump high and far. I could hear him laughing when I would scream. The tarantulas would jump high enough to hit the side of the truck and I was deathly afraid that one would make it into the bed of the truck with me. Uncle Jim knew they couldn't jump that high, but for me, I was living on the edge.

Great Uncle Jim Owen

North Texas Tarantula

I was close to my grandmother and the weeks spent with her in the summers and at other times still hold special memories in my heart. She was a faithful member of the Church of Christ. Not just a Sunday morning member, but a Sunday morning, Sunday night, and most Wednesday night's member. She told me once that she had heard a Church of Christ preacher when she was a little girl and had decided she would be Church of Christ for the rest of her life and she was! I would go to church with her and sit with what seemed like only old people. I remember men in brown suits carrying dress cowboy hats and ladies in long dresses. Everyone would stand and talk and my grandmother would introduce me to everyone every time I came for a visit. Most of the time, after the Sunday night services, one of the old men would take us out for ice cream—another treat I seldom got at home.

Because of this, my grandmother was extremely excited when a young couple moved in next door to my house who just happened to be Church of Christ. Jim and Erma were very nice. Erma was a homemaker and Jim was a salesman and they were just starting their life together. They were also very open to spending some time with me and they were willing to take me to church when I was at home. This absolutely thrilled my grandmother, who wanted me to go every Sunday. For a couple of years, I did go to church with them. I attended Sunday school and was even baptized. The preacher was a nice man. He was excitable and energetic and was evidently well-known for his preaching ability. I don't know if it was through my grandmother or just a twist of fate, but Brother Ramsey ended up being the guest preacher/evangelist at my grandmother's church one week. A week that I just happened to be visiting her. It was a matter of great convenience since he was returning home on a Sunday night and was willing to take me home and save my mother the drive.

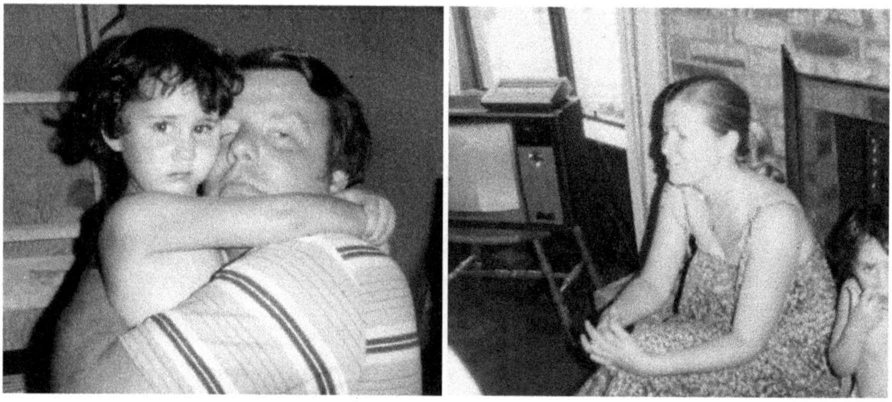

My Neighbors Jim & Erma

I remember talking to him as we drove. I was probably about eight years old at the time and he was asking me what I wanted to do when I grew up. It was a no-brainer for me! I told him I wanted to be a preacher! It was just what I felt I was supposed to do! That trip home should have been uneventful. Little did I know that my life was about to change and not for the better. I had never felt real fear before. As a child, there were things I knew were missing in my life, but I was a fairly sheltered kid. That night I almost died! It was a dark night and a car had broken down on the interstate. It was sitting in the left-hand lane, the one in which we were driving. Brother Ramsey was tooling along about 75 mph, which was the speed limit back then when all the sudden he yelled and swerved his big Pontiac. I guess I was scared by his reaction. He turned all shades of pale and looked like he was going to pass out. He began praying and thanking God we were still alive. He truly believed we almost died and because of what he believed, so did I.

Brother Johnny Ramsey was a Church of Christ preacher who truly exemplified the grace of God in Christ to every person he met. As a small child he impacted my life in ways he never did know before the Lord called him to glory.

It was not long after this event in my life, that everything changed. My life changed and in many ways, my life ended. A journey began which has taken me across the country and around the world in search of something I lost. For thirty-five years, the pain which entered my life and enveloped my heart held me in bondage. I have only now begun to chip away and discover the freedom God truly wants me to experience as His child.

Jesus is able to understand what we endure because He was tempted. ***For because he himself has suffered when tempted, he is able to help those who are being tempted.*** **Hebrews 2:18**

Jesus never experienced molestation as a child, nor did He ever sin Himself. This does not mean He is unable to understand and sympathize with those who do suffer the consequences of sin. The teachings of Scripture are clear in that when Jesus went to the cross He became sin for us: *For our sake he made him to be sin who knew no sin, so that in him we might become the righteousness of God* 2 Corinthians 5:21. This is a difficult passage of Scripture to understand because it seems so unfair. Those who have suffered abuse as children can understand what it means to be treated unfairly and this makes the reality of this passage even more difficult. The Apostle Paul states that Jesus became sin when He was on the cross. Every sin, all sin, rolled into one. Jesus became guilty of all sin as He died, guilty as if He had committed each and every sin. While never guilty in action, He assumed the guilt and with the guilt, He took the shame and the punishment for all sin. He felt what it was like to be both the abuser and the abused, both at the same time. This enables Him to understand what each of us feel in any situation of life. Because of this, He not only understands but is moved to draw close to us and give us His love and assurance for today as well as the future. All are sinful and the effects of sin touch us all.

> ***The earth lies defiled under its inhabitants; for they have transgressed the laws, violated the statutes, broken the everlasting covenant. Therefore a curse devours the earth, and its inhabitants suffer for their guilt; therefore the inhabitants of the earth are scorched, and few men are left.* Isaiah 24:5**

> ***For although they knew God, they did not honor him as God or give thanks to him, but they became futile in their thinking, and their foolish hearts were darkened.***

> *Claiming to be wise, they became fools, and exchanged the glory of the immortal God for images resembling mortal man and birds and animals and creeping things. Therefore God gave them up in the lusts of their hearts to impurity, to the dishonoring of their bodies among themselves, because they exchanged the truth about God for a lie and worshiped and served the creature rather than the Creator, who is blessed forever! Amen. For this reason God gave them up to dishonorable passions. For their women exchanged natural relations for those that are contrary to nature; and the men likewise gave up natural relations with women and were consumed with passion for one another, men committing shameless acts with men and receiving in themselves the due penalty for their error.* **Romans 1:21-27**

The reality of the *fall into sin* (Genesis 4:8) and the rejection of God by all people has brought such corruption upon the world that what was never God's will or desire has become the reality in which we live. Men can be consumed with passion for other men or in some cases, boys. This was never God's plan, nor were human beings designed for this corruption. The very physical design of the human bodies, male and female, reveal God's design and His will. Sin destroyed what was good and pure, and left a tainted shell of what was intended. The ensuing result is that many individuals, who would never reveal what is in the deep recesses of their hearts to adults, will act out their perverted desires on children. It is easy to see why some individuals do such horrible things to others, because it has been this way since the time sin came into the world.

Lessons from Cain & Abel

Let's take a look at the story of Cain and Abel and how it can help us understand some of the dynamics in struggling families today.

> ***Cain spoke to Abel his brother. And when they were in the field, Cain rose up against his brother Abel and killed him.* Genesis 4:8**

Cain was consumed with the selfish desire to be acknowledged in the way Abel was by God. He was jealous and instead of changing his heart and his behavior to be accepted, he chose to act in a way which inflicted harm on the innocent in order to satisfy his own personal selfish desire.

While we may list any number of reasons people grow up to be abusers, the reality is that abusers are psychologically damaged individuals. Abusers generally can be classified as one of three personality disorders: Narcissist, Sociopath, or Psychopath.

Narcissistic Personality Disorder (NPD) is a personality disorder in which there is a long-term pattern of abnormal behavior characterized by exaggerated feelings of self-importance, an excessive need for admiration and a lack of understanding of others' feelings. People affected by NPD often spend a great deal of time thinking about achieving power or success or about their appearance. They often take advantage of the people around them. The behavior typically begins by early adulthood and occurs across a variety of situations.

The **Sociopath** is defined by the DSM-5 as an antisocial personality disorder. It is a pervasive pattern of disregard for and violation of the rights of others, occurring since age 15 years, as indicated by three (or more) of the following:

1) Failure to conform to social norms with respect to lawful behaviors, as indicated by repeatedly performing acts that are grounds for arrest.
2) Deceitfulness, as indicated by repeated lying, use of aliases, or conning others for personal profit or pleasure.
3) Impulsivity or failure to plan ahead.
4) Irritability and aggressiveness, as indicated by repeated physical fights or assaults.
5) Reckless disregard for safety of self or others.
6) Consistent irresponsibility, as indicated by repeated failure to sustain consistent work behavior or honor financial obligations.
7) Lack of remorse, as indicated by being indifferent to or rationalizing having hurt, mistreated, or stolen from another."

Both personality disorders, Narcissistic and Sociopaths, are individuals who were born normal but who suffered severe childhood trauma or neglect which resulted in one of these personality disorders in the individual. No one is born a Narcissist or Sociopath! Each one is made by their environment and then they inflict their poison on the lives of everyone they meet. The majority of child abusers fall into one of these two categories. This coupled with the fact that of the thousands of children who are sexually abused, only about 3% grow up to become molesters themselves, means that each generation is creating its own generation of molesters.

The third psychological disorder is the **Psychopath.** Unlike the Narcissist and the Sociopath, a Psychopath is born with this disorder. Psychopathy is among the most difficult disorders to diagnose. The psychopath can appear normal, even charming. Underneath, the Psychopath lacks conscience and empathy, making the individual manipulative, volatile and often (but by no means always) criminal. Some of the traits of a Psychopath include but are not limited to:

- Lack of remorse or guilt
- Shallow emotions
- Callousness; lack of empathy
- Using others (a parasitic lifestyle)
- Poor control over behavior
- Promiscuous sexual behavior
- Behavioral problems early in life
- Lack of realistic, long-term goals
- Being impulsive
- Being irresponsible
- Blaming others and refusing to accept responsibility
- Having several marital relationships
- Delinquency when young
- Revocation of conditional release
- Criminal acts in several realms (criminal versatility)

The reality is that these three personality disorders are so closely related that it is often difficult for the medical experts to accurately determine and diagnose which one a person suffers from. The truth is that once a person is a Narcissist, Sociopath, or Psychopath, the ability to heal this person is in the hands of God alone. There is nothing modern psychology can do to treat these disorders and reverse them. The individual who suffers from any one of these three personality disorders will be an individual who takes advantage of, uses and abuses other people. The abuse which victims suffer at the hands of individuals with any of these three disorders can generally be narrowed into three general areas: Emotional Abuse, Physical Abuse, and Sexual Abuse. While each of these three areas can be greatly defined into numerous sub-categories, the reality is that the abuse is real and these are the individuals who are doing the abusing.

The long-term effects of abuse upon children range from becoming a narcissist or sociopath, to suffering from PTSD. However, one of the greatest consequences of growing up in an abusive home is the inability to protect the children who are born into your own family. This is generally referred to as having their "Radar Disabled". An individual who grew up having a healthy childhood becomes an adult who is attentive and loving to their own children. When danger is near, this parent will seek to protect their children. An adult parent who grew up in an abusive home, having their radar disabled, will miss the cues most parents see and therefore they will fail to protect their children from the predators who enter into their lives. These are the children who often fall victim to child molesters. Many child advocacy centers across our country are witnessing an alarming pattern. The adults who were once their clients, individuals who suffered sexual abuse as children, are now the parents who are bringing their own children to the centers. As abused individuals, they were unable to identify and protect their children from the abuse they themselves suffered as children.

My own mother, who grew up in an abusive home as a child, was not able to identify danger when it entered into our lives. This opened the way for the predator, who took advantage of the situation in my life.

Chapter Two

The Moment of Truth

The shame and self-hatred I felt kept my secret locked away in the recesses of my heart, while at the same time, it kept everyone out of my heart.

There comes a moment in the lives of most adult survivors when the pain and the shame are too overwhelming to keep bottled up anymore. For me, this moment came when I was entering into a new kind of relationship. I had been in a marriage for more than twenty-five years which was comfortable, but lacked the depth of love and emotional attachment I yearned for in my life. My marriage had ended and I was attempting to move forward in my life. I was struggling to understand who I was and my past was weighing heavily upon me. I did not know then that what I was feeling was what all abuse victims experience. I had met someone and our relationship began simply as friends. We talked and shared ideas and spent time together simply enjoying each other's company. The more time I spent with her, the more I realized I liked her and that for the first time in my life I actually trusted someone. Trusted someone enough to share my secret. I say "share my secret" because I had believed for so many years that if anyone knew my secret I would be rejected and abandoned. The shame and self-hatred I felt kept my secret locked away in the recesses of my heart, while at the same time, it kept everyone out of my heart.

We simply took a drive. I told her I wanted to talk to her and that I had something to share with her about myself that I wasn't sure she would want to know. I was taking a risk. I had lived for years in an empty relationship and I knew if my future and any future relationship was to be different, I would need to learn to be honest—honest with myself and honest with those with whom I desired to share my life. While I wanted honesty, it was honesty that brought real fear into my heart.

As I said, we took a drive—a long drive to an out of the way location where we could sit and talk. We sat in the car, side by side, and I fearfully began to talk around the subject. She assured me that I could tell her anything and whatever it was would not change her opinion of me. They were comforting words on the surface, but down deep I did not believe them! I truly believed that what I had to share would turn her stomach and make me so repulsive in her sight that she would immediately command me to take her home and never contact her again! Such was my fear of being honest with who I was and the past I had lived.

I began telling her that I cared for her and I wanted to be honest and tell her all about my life. I wanted no secrets from her because I cared enough about her to want a friendship with her which was unlike those of my past. She once again assured me it was okay to be honest and that she appreciated what I was doing and that she would not reject me for any reason. Finally, I took the plunge! I actually said it out loud. "I was abused as a child!" ***I WAS ABUSED AS A CHILD!*** The words seemed to stick in my throat. I had feared the worst, but received the best by the grace of God. As she sat next to me and listened to my story, she held onto my arm and my hand. When my eyes filled with tears and my voice quivered she held tight, assuring me that she was still there and that she was not going anywhere. At that moment, I experienced what God had been saying to me for years. I understood unconditional love in a tangible way. I give thanks to God for the gift He sent into my life on that day. A person who could accept me as He does and show me it was safe to be honest with myself and with others concerning my past and the pain it has caused me for so many years. What was true for myself is true for every person who has suffered from abuse, any form of abuse. There needs to be at least one individual to whom the abused person can be honest. A person who will listen to the pain, the heartache, and shame, and who will in the end speak words of truth and comfort to the heart which is fearful and hurting.

That night, sitting in a car, on a lost road in the middle of nowhere, I relayed the sexual abuse I experienced for six years, from ages ten to age sixteen. I was forty-six years old and I had never told anyone of my past. Even though I had feared the worst, I received the greatest gift I have ever experienced in my life. I was accepted for who I was and I was affirmed as someone who was worthy and of value.

This gracious and loving woman that I am referring to is now my wife, Stephanie. She has loved me and accepted me with an unconditional love which has enabled me to continue on the journey I now travel, a journey of healing and wholeness. Because of her personal experiences, she talked

> ***I remember her telling me that "secrets" are given power in the darkness.***

with me about my past and she encouraged me to be honest with myself and others. I remember her telling me that "secrets" are given power in the darkness. Bring all your secrets out into the light, lay them on the table and they will lose their power over you. To a ten-year-old little boy, the secret was powerful and seemingly all encompassing.

When I finally exposed it to the light, the adult in me was enabled to not only accept the truth of what had happened in the past, but to grow beyond the fear which had controlled my life for so long. Stephanie was there for me when I needed to be honest and she accepted me simply for who I was, broken and all. As a result, she has become not only the love of my life but the one person I trust with my whole heart.

I have been very blessed to find a person whom I could trust to tell my secret with and who affirmed me in the midst of my pain. While she had never had any professional training, one of the first statements she made to me when I shared my secret with her was that she believed me. This was followed immediately with the words that she hurt for me. I now know that from a counseling standpoint, she instinctively said the exact words I needed to hear. I am fully aware there are many adult survivors of childhood sexual abuse who yearn for someone like Stephanie to tell their secret to who will believe them and simply hurt with them. You may not have a person like Stephanie in your life at the moment, but there are truly many individuals who understand and are willing to affirm who you are and walk with you through your journey of healing. The world is a different place today than it was when we were enduring the abuse we lived through. Awareness of abuse and both the immediate and long-term effects are understood to a much greater degree than when I was a little boy or even a young adult. We can hardly read the news without seeing an article on abuse and the prosecution of an abuser. Children today face the same danger of abuse, but the difference is that professionals who are in contact with these children, from school counselors to doctors, are more keenly aware of abuse and the potential danger all children face. Help is immediately available to an abused child today with almost every major community having a child advocacy center present. What I want you as my reader to understand is that with this heightened awareness and understanding, there are people in your community to whom you can turn. Many clergy have received specialized training in the area of abuse and can be the first step in assisting you in finding a professional counselor to help you. Your local CPS office will likely have the same list of counselors. You can even turn to the Internet for a listing of counselors who specialize in working with abuse survivors. The point is, you don't have to walk this journey alone. You no longer need to suffer in silence. Help is available for you and I encourage you to take this first step which can change every day of your life from this point forward.

The Challenge

There is another aspect of childhood sexual abuse which directly affects the survivor's ability to make the first outcry for help. It is often not talked about, but I want to address the issue in a very direct way. The issue is a person's gender. When a girl is abused and grows into womanhood and then finds the courage to confront her demons and tell her secret, no one thinks she is any less a woman for the suffering she endured as a child. There is the opposite perception on the part of a man who is a survivor of abuse. The sexual abuse of a boy by another man is a direct attack on everything our society says a man is supposed to be. As an adult, the male survivor assumes the belief that he should have been able to stop the abuse, defend himself, or at least as a man get over it by now. I would venture to say that one of the greatest fears of a male survivor is the belief that others who know him will never look at him the same again. This man believes he will be less of a man if he admits that he was abused. I say this because this is what I believed. I feared Stephanie would reject me because by admitting my abuse, I would no longer be a real man in her eyes. This is a false belief but a belief which male survivors struggle with every day. No rational adult would look at a child who was abused and think any less of that child, male or female, because of happened to them. The child was an innocent victim and bears no responsibility for what took place. The challenge for male adult survivors is that the struggle of the child and the emotions involved with attempting to process the abuse which happened are taking place in the heart and mind of an adult. There is extreme difficulty is separating the two. The adult man relives the abuse with the emotional fear and confusion of the boy. The fear of revealing the abuse stems from the man who has not only hidden the abuse but struggled through life hiding the secret and pretending he is a normal guy like everyone else. The man fears he will be viewed as weak, effeminate, or even have his current sexual identity called into question. If you are a male survivor, please hear what I say. The fear you feel in your heart is real, but it is not valid. Every other male survivor of childhood sexual abuse with whom I have conversed has expressed the same original fear but they have also affirmed the fear was not valid. In fact, the exact opposite has taken place in their lives. The perception of these courageous survivors as men was not diminished but rather enhanced. It is the little boy who fears being found out! It is the man who had the courage to face the abuse, receive the help and support needed to begin the process of healing, and move forward in life. The masculinity of a male survivor of childhood sexual abuse will not be damaged by being honest. The fact is that once the secret is revealed in the light of truth, the survivor is set free to become even more of a man than he was before. Find the help!

Take the chance! You will not regret your decision but just the opposite. You will be set free to become the true man you were created to be.

> ***For who knows a person's thoughts except the spirit of that person, which is in him? So also no one comprehends the thoughts of God except the Spirit of God.*** **1 Corinthians 2:11**

While we may attempt to set it aside or simply put the past abuse out of our mind, it is always there. There is no ignoring it or pretending it did not happen. It was real and it did happen and it was wrong! We may be able to hide the truth from others, but we do live with it every moment of every day. Deep in the recesses of your heart, you know and remember everything and your spirit cries out in pain and grief. Because of this, you live in fear. You fear other people and what they will think of you if they find out your secret. You may even live in fear of God, believing that you are such a damaged person and so unworthy that He does not want you. The abuse survivor spends most of everyday pretending everything is okay, but deep inside he or she knows it is not!

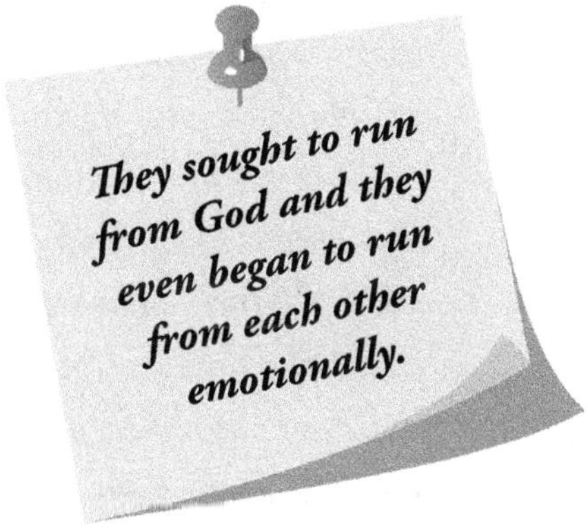

The account of Adam and Eve reveal to us our natural tendency to hide not only our mistakes, but our hurts and shame, even from God.

> ***And they heard the sound of the LORD God walking in the garden in the cool of the day, and the man and his wife hid themselves from the presence of the LORD God among the trees of the garden.*** **Genesis 3:8**

Running away is a natural response for someone who has been abused. Once sin became a reality in the lives of Adam and Eve, they ran. They sought to run from God and they even began to run from each other emotionally. Adam blamed Eve for the action of eating the forbidden fruit and attempted to shift the responsibility. In the case of the abused person, with the abuser nowhere to be found, it is easy to either blame yourself or run away. In my case, I ran away physically for a long time and then when I stopped running physically, I ran emotionally. If there is one thing I have learned, it is that running away does not solve the problem or bring any healing to the hurt. It only prolongs the time it will take for true healing to enter into your life and for real change to take place.

> ***Therefore, since we have been justified by faith, we have peace with God through our Lord Jesus Christ. Through him we have also obtained access by faith into this grace in which we stand, and we rejoice in hope of the glory of God. More than that, we rejoice in our sufferings, knowing that suffering produces endurance, and endurance produces character, and character produces hope, and hope does not put us to shame, because God's love has been poured into our hearts through the Holy Spirit who has been given to us.*** **Romans 5:1-5**

God did not run away from His children, but to them.

If we believe anything about God, then we believe that He knows all things and nothing is hidden from His understanding. Like we said above, Adam and Eve ran away from God, not to God when they sinned. Their guilt and the shame of their sin made them feel unworthy to be with God. But if you notice in the account of Genesis 3, it was

God who came to the garden looking for them. Yes, they had disobeyed God and eaten the forbidden fruit. Yes, they were sinful and now unworthy to stand before a holy God. Yes, there would be consequences in their lives and in our lives as a result of their sinfulness. But none of this changed the love God had for them. He is the one who came looking for them, even though they were sinful. God did not run away from His children, but to them. God came! He came in the garden and He came throughout the history of the world right up to the point Jesus was born! He came to reach out to us and love us, to provide a place of safety and acceptance where real healing can be found. Real healing by knowing and experiencing true unconditional love and acceptance from the One who first loved us! This was the story I told Stephanie that night on the dirt road.

Chapter Three

The New Adventure

All my life I had known my situation was different. My friends in school all had dads at home. In fact, I did not know any other kids with single moms. I knew they were around, but just not connected with my family. My mom worked all the time. She would leave for work a little after ten at night and pick me up from my aunt's house a little after seven in the morning. I would go to school and she would sleep until early afternoon. She would go to her second job at the local drug store and when I got out of elementary school, I would walk to the store to see her and then home to an empty house. I was ten years old at the time! My mom received a phone call one afternoon and called me in from playing outside to give me some bad news. She told me my father had died. I had seen him once and spoken to him on the phone twice during my life. I was extremely sad and cried when she told me. Looking back, I realize it was not sadness because of his death, but sadness at the death of an idea. I had known somewhere out there in the world was a man who was my father. Knowing he was now not there brought a sadness and a sense of being alone. I was even more acutely aware of what was missing in my life when I saw my friends with their dads.

My mother would not need to work her second job very much longer. With my father's death came the death benefits for a minor child. This would allow her to relax and work only one job and still be able to support me. But the next few months would bring changes which would affect the rest of my life.

Before my mother was able to leave her afternoon job, the owner of the store hired a man to be the general manager of the store. After school, I would head across the open field that divided the school yard from the shopping center and into the store to see my mom on my way home. One afternoon she introduced me to a man who had just begun to work in the store. He was nice and seemed to truly like me when we met. Before long, my mother was inviting him over to our house for dinner. For lack of a better way of saying it, they began to date! It was not strange to me, it was exciting. I was able to do things I had never done before. It was October and the State Fair was going on in Dallas. One day he asked if I wanted to go to the state fair. I was excited because I had never gone to a fair before. The three of us went and spent hours on the midway playing the games. I had never had anyone spend money on me and let me have fun like this before. It was a new and exciting experience. For the first time in my life I had a man who was acting like a dad to me. I was experiencing the kind of things my friends did with their dads.

It did not take very long, even before the benefit checks started coming, that he moved into our home. What had started as nights over for dinner soon became much more all seeming so innocent. Instead of having to go across town to my aunt's house, why not just be able to stay at home? He could stay the night while mom went to work! I was excited! Staying at home and no more being in the back bedroom at my aunt's house. I could stay home in my own bedroom and get up in my house and go to school. To top it all off, he was fun to be around. We always had fun, laughing and playing. Now it could go on even longer into the night!

Over the course of a couple of months, my life had changed. I had a "dad" in the home, and I did all the things other kids did with their dads. He liked to grill out and help with dinner. This was great and we would regularly share a big dinner together. This was a far cry from trying to find something for myself to eat while my mom slept in the other end of the house. My kids have a hard time believing that peanut butter sandwiches and pork-n-beans go together, but to a child younger than ten years old, it was easy and quick and at the time it worked for me. What had begun as a unique privilege was now presented as a normal part of an evening at home. When the grill was going, there was usually a beer or two being drank. I was allowed to drink a beer. What a big guy I was! Even my friend's dads did not let them do this. I finally had a "dad" who let me experience special things beyond most boys my age. I remember one time when the three of us were traveling somewhere (I don't even remember where), when he asked for a beer out of the ice chest in the back seat. He wiggled his finger at me and I got a second one out and as I sat in the floorboard of the back seat, I drank beer with my mother a few inches away in the front seat. This was the kind of games we played.

What had been a unique experience at the barbeque grill became a part of every evening. Mom would leave by about ten-thirty at night. Before her headlights were completely out of the driveway, he was headed toward the kitchen for beers. Not just one, but one for him and one for me. I was ten and staying up late drinking beer with a man almost four times my age. These few short weeks were the beginning of the life changing events which marked the beginning of a downward spiral into the abyss of loneliness and shame.

> ***Do not be deceived: Bad company ruins good morals.***
> **1 Corinthians 15:33**

Who is it that we choose to associate with? Is it not people whom we admire and respect? As adults, we choose the people we associate with, but for children this occurs by the choice of others. Add to this that a child is generally very trusting and accepting of adults, especially anyone who will show attention to them. If the adult is a person of good character, the child will begin to emulate these values. If the adult is someone of questionable morals, the child will accept them at least in part. This dynamic stems from the reality that a child who has been unhurt is generally trusting of adults, even to a fault. A child will trust and accept almost without question until pain moves that child to make different choices. Once pain and hurt become part of a person's life that person will begin to run and make different choices, sometimes good and in the case of an abused person, often times bad.

> ***For, speaking loud boasts of folly, they entice by sensual passions of the flesh those who are barely escaping from those who live in error. They promise them freedom, but they themselves are slaves of corruption. For whatever overcomes a person, to that he is enslaved.*** **2 Peter 2:18**

There are few words ever written which are truer. The promise of freedom! The promise of love and acceptance. The promise of fun and adventure. It does not matter what the past circumstances were, the abuser promises that the sky is the limit only in reality to deliver the depths of darkness. I have often wondered what possessed the heart and mind of my abuser to do what he did to me. It is no justification for his actions, but he was enslaved to the corruption of his own heart and desires. He still bore the guilt for the choices he made and the hurt he inflicted, but it was not in him to do differently. He was a corrupted individual. Because of his corrupted heart, he found great pleasure in living out a life which expanded what was in him into the lives of other people. The resulting collateral damage to so many lives was not intentional or even considered as a possibility. Like Cain, the abuser is simply fixated on himself and what he desired with no heart for the consequences in the lives of others.

Chapter Four

The Steep Sliding Slope

It all seemed so innocent, a young boy hungry for the attention of a man and a man who simply wanted to spend time with him. I truly thought he wanted a son as much as I wanted a dad. I quickly found my heart loved him deeply. I had a dad and not just any dad, but a man who wanted to let me experience what grownups did, like sitting in my great-uncle Jim's lap driving his old pickup. I was big now!

Soon, a beer was not enough. We would talk and play, even wrestle on the floor, all things which seemed so innocent. Then, two beers were not enough. Before long, he was letting me experiment with different types of alcohol. We tried wine, whiskey, rum, vodka, tequila, just about anything which could be used to get drunk was used. I was now in junior high and I was going to school with a hangover every single morning. At the worst, I remember sitting on the back porch drinking beer and taking tequila shots, complete with the lime and salt. I was so proud! I did thirteen shots, even more than he did! The sick, sick, hangover did not make me very proud the next morning. Truth is, I don't remember very much about junior high at all. I don't remember my classes or even my teachers. I do remember laying my head on my desk and being sick all the time. There was a lot of drinking, but the alcohol was just a prelude to what he truly wanted.

If alcohol lowers inhibitions, then love lowers resistance. Love opens the way to trust and trust is willing to give someone the benefit of the doubt, even when you don't understand something. I did not understand what happened next, but I loved him and the alcohol made me relax and even enjoy what was happening. It began as simple wrestling and playing. Soon, there was holding and touching and a sense of excitement and even stimulation. I was eleven and just going through puberty. I had experienced an erection and knew that it felt good. The other kids in the neighborhood talked about girls but it was talk with very little that was accurate. But here was a man who was willing to talk about everything, and I do mean *everything.* To pave the way and make things easier, he introduced me to the adventure of porn. An abundance of explicit porn provided excitement for the evenings of drinking. Before long, it seemed like a simple transition from drinking and looking at explicit sex acts between men and women in the magazines to wanting to masturbate while looking at them. He was very encouraging and very willing to help! He wanted me to enjoy the experience, or so he said. So, in a dim lit room, half drunk, with a magazine pulled up close to my face so as not to see what was going on, I felt him take off my shorts and begin to rub on me until I was beyond just sexually excited. I was ready to go all the way!

If alcohol lowers inhibitions, then love lowers resistance.

After it happened, I was not sure I wanted to look at him. I felt a mixed combination of emotions. I was excited and filled with shame. I loved this man I trusted, but at the same time felt that what had just happened was wrong. I was ready for the night to be over, but that was not to be the case. It was a simple statement! He had helped me feel good, so I was now supposed to help him feel good. I remember that I wanted the room very dark. I was scared and sick to my stomach, but I couldn't say no. I remember feeling like I wanted to run away, but I had to do what I felt that I was obligated to do, so I did. This was the beginning!

The next day on the surface seemed like a normal day at school. At least my normal day. I was hung-over like normal and sick until after lunch. When I got home, I was not sure what to expect. It was nearing the holidays and there was a lot of talk about presents and what I wanted for Christmas. Mom fixed dinner and we all ate and I watched TV. When mom left for work, he was eager to break out the booze. I don't remember what the drink of choice was at that particular time, but I know we drank a lot—we always drank a lot. I am not sure if it was that night or simply a night which came very quickly after that first experience, but the next event did come, and it would compound my guilt and shame and cause me to lose myself for many years after.

I don't remember very much. Alcohol numbs you to what is happening at the moment and helps you forget what happened yesterday, at least for a little while. I do remember being very drunk. The idea of sleeping in my bedroom was long gone. I now slept with him in the

Alcohol numbs you to what is happening at the moment and helps you forget what happened yesterday, at least for a little while.

master bedroom from Sunday night through Thursday or Friday night, depending on if mom was getting any overtime or not. We drank all night, looked at numerous porn magazines and masturbated, or at least I was masturbated. He had something more in mind. I remember him telling me to relax. I was too drunk to do much else. He kept telling me to relax and I think I tried, but what I do remember is that I did not like it and I wanted him to stop. He did stop, when he was finished. I laid there for a little while not knowing exactly what to do. I then realized that I needed to go to the bathroom. Here I was, an eleven-year-old boy with the feeling I had to go to the bathroom and get rid of what was inside me. I walked down the hallway, hoping nothing was dripping on the carpet. I locked myself in the bathroom and stayed there for a long time, not really knowing what to do. How do you get something out of your body that is not supposed to be there in the first place? I eventually staggered back to bed and awoke to a normal day of being hungover, but now with new pain—physical and emotional.

This is the man who robbed me of my childhood and abused me for five years.
Rudah Powell
(June 3, 1937 - July 28, 2005)

I was still very young, and I had just entered puberty and I knew nothing about the normal reproduction process. On top of the guilt and shame, I was now afraid. At eleven years old, what was I to think? I knew enough to understand that if two people have sex, there is the likelihood of a pregnancy, right? So, for the next few weeks as things progressed, I truly believed I was going to get pregnant. I was so scared. I lived in fear of what others would think when they found out because you can't hide having a baby. This was the first step I took on the road of feeling the shame of what had happed to me and the beginning of my hiding what had happened to me for fear that others would think I was a bad person because of what I did.

> ***For this reason, God gave them up to dishonorable passions. For their women exchanged natural relations for those that are contrary to nature; and the men likewise gave up natural relations with women and were consumed with passion for one another, men committing shameless acts with men and receiving in themselves the due penalty for their error.*** **Romans 1:26-27**

The Bible speaks of some people becoming so debased that God finally gives them over to the dishonorable or vile passions of their hearts. This is certainly true of the child molester. In many cases, the child molester is involved in sexual relationships with other adults. While there are those who would seek to use the excuse of the "need for sex" to justify the sexual appetite they possess, this is absolutely untrue. A human being is not an animal. We have the ability to control our sexual urges and act appropriately in relation to all people. Because many of these men are already in consenting sexual relationships with other individuals, the drive to have sex with a child comes from a deeper motivation than the simple desire for sex. For the child molester, the desire to have sex is only one facet. The ability to control and manipulate another human being is like an adrenaline rush. The gratification received from this total domination heightens the sexual gratification received. This is one aspect of the corruption of the human heart inside the abuser. To dominate and control is as great a desire as the sexual gratification received. What is true for the child molester is also true for the man who rapes a woman or the husband who

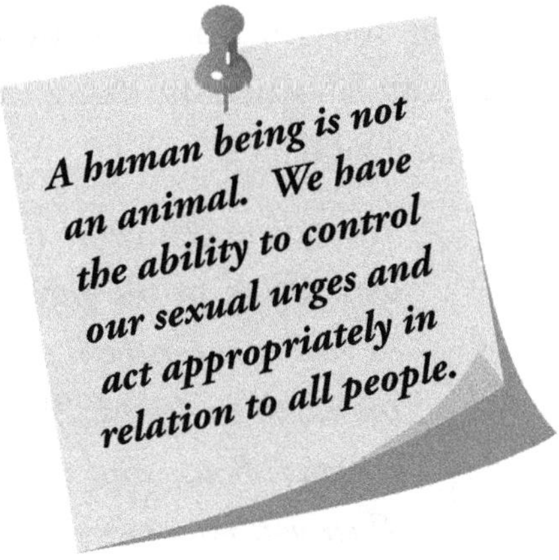

abuses his wife or even the boss who seeks sexual favors from a woman to insure her job security.

Child molestation usually begins with a sex offender gaining a child's trust and friendship. The offender then begins "testing" the child's ability to protect themselves by telling sexual jokes, engaging in horseplay, back rubs, kissing or sexual games. If the child appears comfortable with or curious about this type of behavior, (and most healthy, normal children are) the offender will slowly increase the amount and type of touching to include more direct sexual touching. Child sexual abuse can include exposing, fondling, masturbation, oral sex, intercourse, and pornography. Many children do not understand that what is happening is sexual or wrong. Most offenders know that if they physically harm a child while molesting them, the child is more likely to tell. They are also clever enough to make the child feel as if they are equally responsible for the contact. Children become trapped and are unable to tell anyone what is happening.

> ***The ability to control and manipulate another human being is like an adrenaline rush.***

The following account from Genesis reveals how far the human heart can fall when the desire to obtain what a person wants outweighs all moral guidance.

> ***The two angels came to Sodom in the evening, and Lot was sitting in the gate of Sodom. When Lot saw them, he rose to meet them and bowed himself with his face to the earth and said, "My lords, please turn aside to your servant's house and spend the night and wash your feet. Then you may rise up early and go on your way." They***

said, "No; we will spend the night in the town square." But he pressed them strongly; so, they turned aside to him and entered his house. And he made them a feast and baked unleavened bread, and they ate. But before they lay down, the men of the city, the men of Sodom, both young and old, all the people to the last man, surrounded the house. And they called to Lot, "Where are the men who came to you tonight? Bring them out to us, that we may know them." Lot went out to the men at the entrance, shut the door after him, and said, "I beg you, my brothers, do not act so wickedly. Behold, I have two daughters who have not known any man. Let me bring them out to you and do to them as you please. Only do nothing to these men, for they have come under the shelter of my roof." But they said, "Stand back!" And they said, "This fellow came to sojourn, and he has become the judge! Now we will deal worse with you than with them." Then they pressed hard against the man Lot and drew near to break the door down. But the men reached out their hands and brought Lot into the house with them and shut the door. And they struck with blindness the men who were at the entrance of the house, both small and great, so that they wore themselves out groping for the door. **Genesis 19:1-11**

The men of Sodom wanted to rape the two men (angels) who had arrived at Lot's house. These men of the city had no regard for the well-being of anyone but themselves. They were willing to take by force what was not theirs to obtain. It is not that there were not women or even other willing men in Sodom. The city was as devoid of morals as any modern city of today. These men desired to take, with force and control what they wanted. This reveals the condition of the hearts of these men. There was more to their desires then sexual gratification. There was a desire to control and dominate which fueled their sexual desires.

Chapter Five

Isolation

There were rapid changes taking place since "he" had entered my life. Now, I was always too busy on the weekends to go to church with Jim and Erma. There was never any time to go see my grandmother. I dropped out of scouts and all extra activities at school. I never went to my friends' houses anymore. There were always too many things we wanted to do together and there was no time for anyone else. This was even quickly becoming true for my own mom. More than once, the conversation between he and I was about how the week nights were so much better than the weekends when mom was home. These conversations generally took place late in the evening when we were drinking and talking about all the things we could do alone for fun.

He began to expand my experiences by taking me to meet friends of his. I remember a young guy named David. He was young in comparison to my abuser. David was in his late twenties and he lived with his parents who were quite well off. He had a neat room attached to his parent's house. It was complete with black lights and a full bar. I would sit with the big boys and talk, drink and watch movies like I had never seen before. From lifeless still shots to full action, these were X-rated movies. I would watch these movies and want to experience the satisfaction of an orgasm. My abuser never let anyone else touch me, but he would put me out there on display as it were. David was also the source for pot. We added this to our normal routine. We would drink, smoke pot, look at magazines or watch movies and have sex. Perverted as this sounds, this became my life even before the first holiday season was over.

I mention the holidays because there was a major focus on *things* that year. He was fairly handy and he made me something and brought it to me. It was a large Christmas boot, made from wire and covered with felt. It was made to look like a boot Santa would wear. It was about three feet tall and had an opening in the top about a foot in diameter. He placed several small presents in the boot with the goal to fill the boot by Christmas. But the game each night was for me to empty the boot and count how many presents were in the boot and work as hard as I could at begging to be allowed to open just one more early. This went on each night for the whole month of December. Reflecting on these events, I now realize he was using *things* to buy my love, or at least my silence.

That Christmas saw the onslaught of more presents then I ever thought was possible. My mother was never able to give me very much, but that particular year I received more presents than anyone else I knew. And to top it all off, he gave

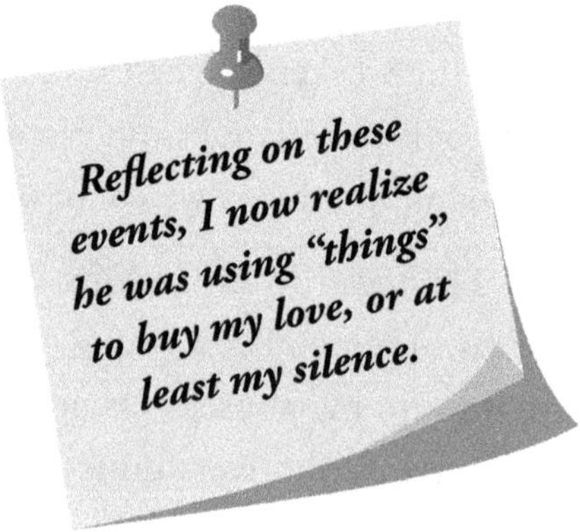

me a shotgun. A real, honest to goodness shotgun which he promised to take me to shoot as soon as we could find a place.

The day after Christmas, we loaded up in the car and began to drive, looking for a place for me to shoot my new gun. It seems strange now, but we drove for three hours from Dallas to a small town in central Texas. A long way to go just to shoot a gun. We asked a man at the local convenience store if there was any place we could shoot a new gun. He was a nice young man who said his dad had a farm just outside of town and he would let us shoot there. This one trip would open up a whole world of hopes and hurts in my life.

Chapter Six

A Double Life

As strange as it sounds, the farm became a double-edged sword in my life. It was the perfect excuse to escape from my mom on the weekends. And I do mean *every* weekend. We would load up the truck on Friday afternoons and head out for the three-hour drive. We would arrive late evening and the party would begin. For a while, we would camp out, but before long it became much easier to simply rent a room in the local motel. There were certainly more comforts, such as a TV and a real bed instead of a cot. The motel ice machine ensured that the mixed drinks would continue to flow. There were a few occasions that I was allowed to take friends along, but this made things difficult. It was not easy to continue with our normal routine unless my friends got extremely drunk and passed out which did happen on occasion.

During the day, the old man on the farm taught me about cattle and horses and what it meant to be a cowboy. I learned how to ride and train horses, which would serve me well in the future. When I bought a mare, he even showed me how to care for her hooves and shoe her. There wasn't anything about working with animals the old man did not want to teach me. His own grandsons were little and his children were grown. I guess I was a fill-in grandson until his got older. Since I had never had a grandfather, he was great. I have nothing but good memories of this old gentleman cowboy. The farm provided a place to play in new ways. What began as a place to simply shoot a gun became a standard home away from home. Every weekend I was there riding, shooting, exploring, having fun throughout the day. Each night the drinking and everything else took place.

The farm gave me a place to learn and grow. A place to explore and be a kid.

L. M. Martin was a true cowboy.
A man of integrity whom I respected. Like a grandfather, he taught me life lessons I value to this day.

After a few months of this, things began to change at home. I am not sure exactly what, but all of a sudden my abuser was moving out and I was asked to choose who I wanted to live with—him or my mom. For me, it was no choice. I chose him. We moved from the house I had lived in all my life to his sister's house with her husband and family. She was a very likable person, but looking back I realize things were very strange. She was home every day and her boys were both in school. Her husband was a salesman and was gone during the day and home every night. We were given a room for the two of us and she always expected us for dinner before we went out. We did begin going out every night. When I would come in before supper she was always ready to give me a hug and a kiss. I was turned on by her and would look for opportunities to get additional hugs and kisses. I had never kissed a woman on the lips, but I did her and quite often. I was now around thirteen and noticing girls in a big way. She would hug me and give me a kiss that was longer than just a peck. It was something I looked forward to every day.

Our routine changed. The weekends were still spent on the farm, but Sunday through Thursday nights were spent at her house. I never remember seeing or even talking with my mom for the months we were gone. What I do remember is that we needed to get out of the house to do the heavy drinking so my horizons were expanded once more.

Chapter Seven

New Horizons

I am not sure I can remember the order of places we experienced, but I do remember them all. There were the regular bars where we would drink and play pool. I wasn't a bad pool player so I was given my own pool cue and case. I thought I was the little big man going into a bar at ten o'clock at night to play pool with the pool sharks. We would drink and shoot pool until the early hours of the morning and then stagger into his sister's house to our room for the evening activities. I would get up in the morning, hung over and sick. I would go to school and sit with my head on my desk until lunch and then by the afternoon, I was ready to go again. Each night we would usually return to the same place, a place where he could get by calling himself my dad and getting me in the door.

When one place became boring, we would find another. I was very excited to go to the strip clubs. It was a phase we went through. It was a little tougher to get by the bouncers, but he could always find a club for us to go to. We would sit and watch the ladies dance and one time, when I was good and drunk, he gave me a handful of dollar bills and told me to go for it. The ladies would dance to the edge of the stage and pull back their G-strings and let me put the money in. Then, the unexpected happened. One lady pulled my face into her breasts and rubbed herself all over my face. All the men began to hoop and holler and clap for me. I was once again the center of attention and I liked it! This went on until it became too routine and it was time for another adventure.

One night, he decided we should go to a new bar, one we hadn't been to. I didn't care! It was the same wherever we went. Too much drinking and a lot of him talking to other guys and I would play pool or talk to, or at least look at the ladies. Sometimes if there was a dance floor, I would even dance with some of the ladies. On this one night, we went to a bar that had a pool table and as usual I began to shoot pool with the guys there. The normal rule was that you put your quarter on the table in line to have a turn. Each new player would play the winner of the previous game. Once I got on the table, I was allowed to play continuously. It took me a while to actually catch on. This bar had no ladies in it. My abuser sat at the bar laughing and talking with the guys who were gathered around. They would all watch me and cheer for me when I would make a good shot. But, win or lose, I continued to play. It was only after a while that I realized we were in a gay bar and I was the focus of attention for every man in the place. Looking back, I realize I was put on display like a trophy. He paraded me around to let everyone see he had a young boy at his beck and call and he would be the one who took me home when the bar closed. I guess he was the big man for the evening. All night long the men wanted to play pool with me. I remember one black man who was eager to talk to me and spend time playing pool. I realize now that he had more interest than playing pool, but my abuser would never let anyone else touch me. I was totally his and his alone.

I am not sure exactly what happened, but after a few months we moved back to the house with my mom. Everything resumed as if we had never left. Only now, we would sometimes stay at home for our drinking and other activities and sometimes we would venture out to the bars.

Chapter Eight

On the Road

Somewhere in the mix of all these events, he went to work for an old friend of his. He owned a company which distributed large brass valves, the kind used in factories and in the oil fields. West Texas was the territory he was assigned, so off we would go each week to a different area of West Texas. I know he made calls on businesses, but I don't remember anything about it. It was summertime so I was with him full time. Each day was a different town and a different motel. A green Cadillac and an expense account credit card. What a life. Different bars and night clubs each evening and all the drinking and porn we wanted. In the daytime, I often slept in the car as we traveled from town to town. Not so different than when I was in school. By lunchtime, I

would begin to feel better and I would be raring to go by the evening. We would return home on Thursday or Friday, only to turn around and head out to the farm again. We had moved back home, but not really. I was always gone. I never saw my mother or any other members of my family, or any of my old friends. He had me all to himself and for a time, that was all right with me.

Chapter Nine

Hard Changes

Picture taken 4 years prior to leaving home

The life I was living from age ten through fourteen was an abnormal normal. What would be simply out of the question as a way of life for most people was normal for me. Along the way, we experimented with almost every type of alcohol and different types of drugs. We spent more time with his friends and a lot of time on the farm. I entered high school at the age of fourteen. As a freshman, I was doing what most college kids experience when they first leave home. I did become involved in FFA and showed animals for a couple of years. I made it through my freshman year even though I did not do very well in school. I barely passed most classes and actually failed English. My sophomore year continued on about like my freshman year with the exception I was taking freshman English along with sophomore English. I passed freshman and failed sophomore English! This was repeated the next year—passed sophomore and failed junior English. At age fifteen, I discovered something. I really liked girls. If anyone had ever told me

I was gay or a homosexual, I would have killed them. I never viewed myself this way and I knew I wasn't. I liked girls and wanted to have a girlfriend all the time. I know now that I was searching for someone to affirm my manhood. At fifteen, I bought an old pickup from one of the boys on the farm and I would spend every afternoon working on it. When I began to drive with a permit, I wanted to go everywhere like every other teenager. He didn't want me to. He didn't like the girlfriends I had. They were never good enough. He could always find something wrong with them, which he very much enjoyed pointing out to me. Like most teenagers, I would spend a great deal of time talking on the phone. When he would come home from work, if I was on the phone he would tell me to hang up and get off the phone. This was long before the days of cell phones or even cordless phones. My house had a phone stand built into the wall in the hallway outside my room. The cord was just long enough to reach inside my room and close the door. I would lie on the floor with the receiver to my ear and talk to my girlfriend. It became a normal episode for him to open the door and kick me and tell me once again to get off the phone. This was the prelude to the changes which were coming in my life.

When I was sixteen and began to drive on my own, the real problems started. I would come and go as I pleased. I got a job and began working a lot of weekends which made it difficult to go to the farm as we had done for so long. Instead, I was wanting to go out on dates and hang out with my friends. This made him very angry. What would begin as an evening of excitement about a night out with my girlfriend, would end up in an all-out fight in the hallway outside my bedroom. He would pick and jab and say negative things about the girl I was dating. He would call them horrible names, such as slut and whore just to make me angry. When I had heard enough, I would want to leave. He would block the door and refuse to let me out of my room. When I pushed him out of the way, the fight was on. Picture, if you will, a forty-three-year-old man fighting a sixteen-year-old. When I finally did get out of the house, I was usually bleeding and my shirts were often torn. Not exactly ready to go out on a date. Most girls were scared away by all of this, but a few understood and continued to date me. When I would get home, he would be there, ready to have a drink and apologize. This was especially true if it was a weeknight. He would want to sit down and drink for a while and talk. He would play nice and after several drinks, everything seemed to be alright. This pattern went on for a while and I began to become suspicious of what was taking place. One night, I did not drink as much as I let on. I wanted to stay somewhat sober and find out what was happening. I was right! He guided me to my bedroom, where I had actually been sleeping for a few months. Once I was in bed, he left, only to return shortly preparing to rape me in a drunken stupor. I realized this is what had been happening for months and the rage that whelmed up inside me was all consuming. I reached across to my dresser where I had a pistol that he had bought me a few years before. I cocked it and placed it in the middle of his face. He froze and was horrified that I was not passed-out drunk. I told him to get off my bed and out of my room and if he ever touched me again, I would kill him. I meant what I said, and he knew it. He hurried out of the room and then life fell apart!

Ruger .357 Blackhawk

Over the next few weeks the fighting became even more frequent. My mother was freaking out, not knowing what was going on or what to do. I stayed gone as much as I could but when I did go home it was always a fight. I had just finished my junior year. I passed all my courses except, of course, English. I remember sitting in my room crying, not knowing what to do. I had no one to talk to, and no one I felt that I could turn to for help. The friends I did have were only a couple of years older, ones I had made since I began driving and gaining some measure of independence.

I want to pause for a moment and make an observation or at least for me, a realization from my past. From the end of my sixth-grade year when the drinking and abuse started, through the end of my junior year in high school, I was pretty spaced out in school. I was hung over almost every day, sick with my head on my desk. I did no homework and I barely passed the classes I did pass. In that span of five years, I never had one single teacher ask me about my home life. I know I must have appeared hung over and I probably smelled like booze, but no one questioned anything. My mother was never called for a consultation, nor was I ever sent to the nurse's office or a counselor's office. There is a responsibility on the part of adults who are involved in the life of a child to inquire when something does not seem right. Add to this that my extended family, who were living in the same town and never sought to understand what was taking place compounded the anger I felt as a young adult who was struggling alone in silence. The decades leading up to the late 70's were years when abuse was prevalent, but silence prevailed. The nightly news gave no reports of abusers being arrested and families who experienced multiple forms of abuse kept quiet. Society in general did not want to know about abuse and it was hidden away from the public leaving the victim to suffer along. Thankfully, we are beyond those years, but for the victim who was failed by family and teachers in the past, there is an ingrained sense that the abuse should still be kept hidden and the silence never broken. This leaves the person who was abused to suffer in silence. Unfortunately, there were no adults in my life who I knew well enough or could trust with my secret. I had nowhere to turn, so I sat by myself in my room with that same pistol in my hand which I had used to threaten my abuser. I had it loaded and cocked. It was a Ruger .357 Blackhawk. I remember staring down the barrel, seeing the tip of the bullet which was ready to do the job it was intended to do. It would have made a huge mess if I had pulled the trigger. That is the only reason I didn't. I did not understand the dynamics of abuse so at that point I didn't blame my mother and I did not want her to have to be the one to find me and clean up the mess that I would leave behind if I did pull the trigger. I held the gun in front of my face looking down the hole of the barrel for a long time before I lowered the hammer. I was dying inside and I knew I could not go on another day enduring the life I had been living.

I threw some jeans and shirts in a bag and loaded all my guns in my truck—by this time I had several. I climbed in the truck and drove away. I drove away from everything and everyone I knew. It would be a year and a half before I would return home. I was looking for a safe haven and thankfully I found one.

Chapter Ten

The Ranch

I drove for a long time that afternoon. I headed South, which was the direction of the farm, but I knew I didn't want to go there because it would create too many questions and there would be too much to explain. The family there, who had befriended us, believed I was his son and I didn't know how to tell them I wasn't or even why I was there by myself. On several occasions, I had seen a horse ranch off the highway as we traveled to the farm. As I got closer to the ranch, I began to think that maybe I could stop and see if I could get a job. It was fortunate for me that when I pulled in, the owner was there. He didn't live at the ranch but only visited a couple of times a week. His name was Mr. Thompson and he owned a big factory in Ft. Worth. His son had taken over the operation leaving him to run and play as he wanted to do. He had purchased several retired race horses and was setting up a breeding barn. I happened along at the right time. Stallion Alley was ready to open for business and they needed an extra hand.

Mr. Thompson owned thirteen stallions and over two hundred mares. He would breed the mares and then when the foals were born, he would begin the process of culling. Those who looked to have the potential for racing he would sell to people who were seeking to make a name in the race horse industry. The colts which would not make good race horses would run free and untouched until they were about two years old. I arrived when the first crop of two-year-olds needed to be broke and trained for pleasure riding.

Sandi, the ranch foreman asked me several questions and Mr. Thompson chimed in on occasion. They decided to hire me for a while and see if I really did know anything about horses. Since Stallion Alley was open for business, there was a steady stream of visitors who were bringing mares to be bred to one of the thirteen stallions stabled there. This, along with the training of the two-year-olds kept me very busy. Sandi liked the way I did not give up when working with the fillies. Normally, if I had actually trained the horses the way I wanted, I would have taken a great deal of time with them to gentle them down before ever attempting to ride them. Mr. Thompson had different ideas. He wanted them saddle broke and sold as soon as possible. This meant working as a rodeo cowboy every day. I would rope a filly and tie her to the fence, eventually getting an actual halter on her. I would leave her tied for most of the day, spending time petting her and talking to her. This was the first time many of these horses had ever been touched. I would eventually get a bridle and saddle on them and once my seat hit the saddle, the show was on. People driving down the highway would stop on the side of the road to take pictures. Things were not as they should have been. The corral was square, not round. Things were rushed instead of taking the time to do it right, but I really didn't care. When I was thrown, I got up and tried again. When a horse would run me into the pipe fence, I just got back on and held on. I remember one filly that simply did not want me on her back. She would rare up, dance backwards and flip, landing on her back, on me and the saddle. I always managed to clear the saddle, but not always her. If she could get me off without flipping, which she was good at, she would not run away, rather she would turn and attack me. She would rare and stomp, trying to keep me on the ground. I was stomped and kicked a lot by her and a few others. But I didn't care. As I look back, I realize that while I was unable to pull the trigger when I was sitting in my room, my desire to die had not diminished. I didn't care about life, so I didn't care what happened to me along the way. This was a feeling I would carry with me for the next thirty years.

I want to tell you a little bit about Sandi Russell. She was a flower child of the 60's. She had lived free and unhindered all her life. She was emotionally close to her parents, but I always felt she was estranged. She lived alone in the ranch house which she reluctantly agreed to share with me when I was hired on. I would like to think we became friends for a time. She was lonely and I was hurting. She did not pry into my past and I did not pressure her in the present. She was a person who had lived a hard life but she had a soft heart. She knew something was wrong in my past, but she didn't pressure me to talk. She simply let me be who I wanted to be, which was what I needed at the time. I had skipped my senior year so when school began the next year she did insist that I at least go locally for my senior year. I tried, but it didn't work out very well. We would spend our days working the horses and doing all the chores of the ranch. A couple of times a week, we would drive into the small town nearby to eat at the diner. She loved to do this and I think she was glad not to be eating alone. She let me hurt and grieve in private but was always ready to simply shoot the bull and spend time together. When I left the ranch to return home, I did so rather abruptly. Not in anger, but it was just time to go! I had finally gone home to see my mom for a weekend. I linked up with some old friends who were now graduated and more importantly I had found out that my abuser was no longer living with my mother. I thought I could go home and all would be good again. My mistake.

Sandi had me dress up and ride one of the stallions from the ranch in the local county fair parade.

Chapter Eleven

You Can Never Really Go Back Home

I'm not sure I ever really understood the phrase "you can't go back home", until I lived it. Things were different. I was a high school drop out with no direction and only a desire to do as I pleased. I may have felt this way since I had been controlled for so long by him and being back in the same house, I was feeling anxious all the time. I went out dancing with some friends and ran into a girl I knew from high school. We literally backed into each other on the dance floor. I talked to her for a while and before long, we began to date. This all seemed normal and good, but then things turned south again. Before I knew what happened, *he* moved back into my mom's house. I could not believe that she let him back in. I was horrified. I wanted to strangle someone. All I knew is that I had to get out. One of the difficult dynamics of abuse victims which few understand is the emotional control the abuser possesses. Being in the same room with the person who abused you sends you back to being a little child. I felt helpless and alone in the darkness with my secret. There was a raging war inside of my heart. The struggle between loving the man who was the only dad I had ever hand and the hate fueled anger of a victim combined with the helplessness of suffering alone in the silence. I could not stay! I could not tell! So I chose the only course of action I believed I had. I chose to run, again!

One of the first things he did was to begin to rag on the girlfriend I had and I was not going to take it. Fights ensued again and I was determined to get out. I asked my girlfriend to move in together in an apartment and she agreed. At least I was out, but things did not change very quickly or in a very good way.

He had controlled my life for so long, I was determined never to allow him to do it again. I was eighteen. I had been gone for over a year and a half, living on the ranch. I was now back home trying to start over and he was attempting to buy his way into my life again. I did not want him or his money. I wanted a life on my own and the only way I knew for sure to get rid of him was to do extreme things which he disapproved of and which would move me toward full independence from him. I asked my girlfriend to marry me.

I asked her to marry me because I knew he did not want me to. I was eighteen and working a decent job. We were living together and it seemed to be the natural thing to do. Besides, it made him mad which was a bonus for me. The girl I was dating said yes and we set the date. My mother was not involved in the planning of the wedding at all since he was still in the picture. The day finally came, and the wedding was nice. I was scared to death, not really knowing or understanding what I was doing. He was not invited to the wedding, but he came anyway. At the reception, which was held in the club house of our apartment building, he was present in all his pomp and circumstance. Before the cake was cut or the punch was served, he picked a fight with me in front of all our guests. My best man and groomsman pulled us apart and sent my wife and I on our way. In other words, we missed our own wedding reception. Such was the beginning of my life as a married man. It was a journey which would take me to great heights and even greater depths.

Chapter Twelve

From Newlyweds to a Silver Anniversary

From this point forward in my life, I begin to see things improve or so I thought. One of my longtime friends who was one of the groomsman in my wedding invited us to come to a Bible study group at his church. He said it was a group of young adults, couples and singles, who simply loved to hang out and do things. I was looking, searching for something, and I didn't even know what it was. The first few months of marriage were not what I had expected. It was not necessarily bad, but I guess I had hoped for more. The relationship with my wife seemed superficial. I wanted something deeper and more meaningful. I was yearning to connect on an intimate level, which was not happening. We had rushed into marriage and I soon found that I was looking elsewhere for affirmation. One afternoon, I was in the pool at the apartment when two girls came for a swim. Before long we were all flirting and I was ready and willing to go to their apartment with them, which did not happen, because I had been married less than three months. When my friend invited us to the young adult group, I said yes, even though my wife didn't really want to go.

The group turned out to be exactly what my friend had described. A group of about fifteen to twenty young adults, some single and some married, who would hang out, study a lesson, and do things together. What began as a Saturday night group, expanded to a broader group within the church and this group began to take on a life of its own. The leader was hired as a full-time staff member of the church and several of us began to be groomed as leaders in the church. I was not new to church, but I was new to seeing church done this way. There was music and singing, multiple people leading Bible studies, and I could do anything I wanted to do and was asked to do several things. I found a great deal of affirmation from members of the church and when it came to the Bible studies, I was like a sponge soaking everything up.

One of the many trips our Young Adult Bible Study group took.

After the wedding fiasco, my abuser was finally and truly gone from my mom's house, but that did not matter, I had a new life now. I drug my wife along to every bible study and event that the church hosted. It actually got to the point that going to the church was an everyday event and having a regular job got in the way of serving God. I decided it was time to have a talk with the pastor about my dilemma. He was nice enough and explained all my options. My wife had encouraged me to get my high school diploma, which I did at a night school. So, when the pastor began talking about positions of service in the church, I was ready and able to consider each one. He mentioned everything you can imagine, except being a pastor. I was naive enough to ask what it took to be a pastor. He said eight years of schooling, minimum. I popped off, "I can do that" and in my mind, all was set for me to become a pastor. I quit my full-time job, got a part time job at a local Christian bookstore and enrolled in a local Bible college. I chose the Bible college because I could get my language requirements for the seminary.

It was about this time that my wife informed me that she was pregnant. My mother was supportive of my going to school and even of the idea of going to seminary. She was happy for me because I seemed happy. In many ways, I was happy. I was doing well in school and I had a goal. For the first time I knew what I wanted to do, something I actually wanted to do, or so I thought.

Chapter Thirteen

Full Time Student, Part Time Job & A Child on the Way

I discovered very quickly that if you performed well, people would respond with a great deal of affirmation. I was doing very well in school and with a baby on the way, my mother did not want me to slow down on my studies. She offered to let my family move in and share her house. My wife and I did this and a few months later, we had a baby girl. I remember wondering what I was supposed to do. What does it mean to be a dad? I never really had a dad, not one I would want to emulate in any way.

I continued to do well in school and I enjoyed my work in the bookstore and everyone was proud of what I was doing in my life. My life had all the appearances of success, but inside I was extremely empty. The relationship with my wife slipped into a mutually supportive, comfortable relationship which lacked any depth. This would be the status quo of our relationship for the next twenty years together.

Life was extremely busy as I neared the end of my college days. The college was on a semester system while the seminary was on a trimester system. I was set to graduate in December and seminary classes began in September, December, and March. I was desperate to begin the December quarter and in no way wanted to wait until March. My professors agreed to allow me to finish my papers early and take my exams two weeks before the semester ended and leave for seminary by the first of December. This was almost unheard of, but as I said, I had done very well in college. I was taking twenty-one hours and I worked extremely hard to finish all my assignments and prepare for exams. I took tests all day on the Tuesday and Wednesday before Thanksgiving. When I walked out of the building on Thanksgiving Eve, I was finished with college. Monday morning, I would be sitting in my first seminary class. The only challenge was to move from Dallas to St. Louis over the weekend.

I am eternally grateful for the quality of Biblical Education I received both at Dallas Christian College & Concordia Seminary, St. Louis

Chapter Fourteen

A Seed Bed for Learning -Not for Growth

I remember the excitement and the overwhelming sense of awe when I walked onto the seminary campus as a student for the first time. I quickly got busy with reading and writing assignments. My wife went to work at the church headquarters which were also in St. Louis. Our daughter was two and went to daycare at a Montessori school run by a professor's wife. All seemed very good in my life but my relationship with my wife was floundering in a very bad way and I didn't have anyone that I felt I could tell. Can a seminary student, a perspective pastor, have any real problems? Can a pastor have problems in his personal life? Heaven forbid!

It does not take the average student very long to realize that everything which happens at the seminary is evaluated and logged for future reference. When a small group of men will be determining your future, you watch very closely what you say and do. My wife and I were living together on our own for the first time in a long time, with no one else around. When I was busy with schoolwork all seemed good. When it was just us, something was missing. I was empty on the inside. I wanted more and she didn't have any more to give.

We went to counseling for the first time when we were in St. Louis. I was assured the seminary would never find out! I was the one who wanted to go to counseling. In fact, each and every time we went to counseling, I was the one who insisted on it and almost had to force her to go. I don't remember very much about the counseling, except that it accomplished nothing. How could it? The real issues were deep inside me and I was not even acknowledging that I had any issues in my life.

Classmates - Friends during seminary years

When the counseling proved to be a waste of time, we just trudged on in our course. There were always papers to write, books to read, sermons to prepare and people to impress. The word "seminary" means "seed bed". The idea is that it would be a place of Christian education and personal spiritual growth. It did prove to be a place of learning and learning in the highest degree, but it was not a place of growth! If anything, seminary, for me, proved to be a place where the need to impress others and appear to have life under control was much more important than being honest. It was a training place for the art of facade. To be honest about your life and your struggles could get you sent home! Everyone had to learn to hide who they truly were on the inside—something I was already very good at! Another baby, graduation, placement and we were off to serve God full time. Or at least play the game very well!

Chapter Fifteen

Who Shepherds the Shepherd

The devil came to me disguised as more,
One more good thing I could do,
Should do,
And then another,
And another.
I was seduced and misguided.
The more sapped my energy, my joy, my delight.
There was more harshness and impatience
In my voice and my presence.
And the devil grinned,
While God sighed patiently
Knowing that when I get worn down enough,
I'll come home to my true self,
To being my true self in God.

– Clarence Heller, "More"

Used with Permission

Please don't get me wrong. I truly love serving God as a pastor in the church. Truthfully, I can honestly say, I have been pretty good at it. I am a good preacher and teacher and I have given sound biblical counseling to hundreds of people over the years. I have done all I was supposed to do and in many cases much more, all the time as one who is unworthy and disconnected from the message I proclaimed.

The desire to die morphed into a settled understanding that I did not deserve to live a long life. In fact, I felt that I was supposed to die at a relatively young age. What I believed and taught as true for others, I actually believed to be true. God is real and His grace and forgiveness in Christ are free to everyone through simple faith. The gospel, the good news, is pure and free to everyone who wants it! I believed this and I preached this with gusto! It was simply not to be for me. What I knew and believed was true for the whole world was not going to be for me because I did not deserve it!

The sad truth is that I was okay with this reality. I would be used by God to touch the lives of countless people with the message of His love and I would assure them of forgiveness and life at no cost to them. Then, I would die at a young age and go to hell. It all seemed perfectly logical and normal to me!

I have since come to realize that the desire to die that was present when I was sixteen and sitting with a gun in my hand never really went away. It was always there, just under the surface of my life and my heart. Because I did not deserve to be loved, I did not know what it meant to love others. Because I needed to be constantly affirmed as to who I was and that I was of some value, I worked harder than anyone else so as to be affirmed. My life and my sense of self identity became performance based in every way. This was all fine and good when I was out serving others in the church, but when I returned home each evening, there was a deep emptiness which longed to be filled.

I should stop and tell you a little about my first wife. She was raised in less than desirable circumstances. She was distant from most people and very closed emotionally to affection, either giving or receiving. This compounded the difficulties I struggled with since I desired for someone to affirm me through loving and accepting me for who I was not based on what I did. Unfortunately, she was unable to do this, not because she did not want to affirm me, but because she did not know how to do this in herself. She always had a low self-esteem and she developed a pattern of becoming very critical as a defense mechanism. This proved to be a very difficult combination for me in my personal life. I was always looking for affirmation through some deeper emotional connection. She was always distant emotionally and critical when I expressed my desire for more closeness. If I would simply settle for the status quo of a relationship where we could be like best friends, everything would be alright. If I pushed for more, she became defensive which caused me a great amount of anger and heartache.

There were two times when I came very close to ending my relationship with her. The first was when I was at the second church I served. I was living in a small town in the middle of Texas and while successful in the church and community, I felt like an utter failure in my own home. I sat down and wrote a letter of resignation to the church. This is a quote from that letter:

> ***How can I lead the people of God when I am a failure in my own house? People turn to me for help and guidance and I speak the truth but in turn I am unable to apply the same truth within the four walls of my own home. The one thing I have always said is that a pastor must have integrity. If he loses this one quality he***

will certainly bring disgrace upon the Church of God. I have lost what little integrity I have sought to establish because I have been unable be what I have proclaimed to be, a husband and a father.

I never acted on the letter I wrote that day in 1998. Years later, I wrote a similar letter while at my next parish. I was nearing the end of my proverbial rope when a close and dear friend took me away for a week to clear my head. I returned and served for another six years before learning to be honest with myself. The result of learning to be honest with myself has led me to deal with my past and it has changed my future. It has not been easy, but it has been real and it has been honest.

Chapter Sixteen

The Next Step-
Beyond the Dirt Road

That night sitting in the car on the dirt road, telling my story for the first time to Stephanie, opened up a whole new world to me. I now knew it was okay to be honest and that this huge secret did not need to be so scary anymore. The more I talked with Stephanie about my past the more I was convinced that I should tell others around me so that this huge division in all my relationships could be healed. I made the hard decision that it was time for me to tell my mother. I knew it would be a difficult conversation and that she would need support when our talk was concluded. Because of this, I decided to tell my sister first. She lives some distance from the town I lived in and it would have to be a phone conversation. Not exactly what I wanted to do. It is hard to speak of difficult things over the phone when you are fearful of how people will react. You lose the ability to read the emotions of facial expressions and body language. As I told her of my past, she did express sympathy and compassion for me. She is quite a bit older than I am so she knew my abuser as an adult. She said she did not know what had taken place, but that she and her husband did not like the man and that they had always felt that something was not right. Looking back, I see this as one more missed opportunity of intervention which could have changed the course of my life at an earlier point. She saw and questioned, but did not act. While I felt let down by my sister, my purpose for calling was the concern I had for our elderly mother and how she would take the news and she assured me she would be ready to talk to her when I had finished telling her.

I approached my conversation with my mother with no little amount of fear. I never doubted that my mother loved me the best way she could. I understand now that because of her own childhood she was unable to see the warning signs of abuse when it entered her own home. I felt love for my mother, but it was a love which was distant and filled with confusion and anger. I knew what I was about to share with her would be extremely painful and hard to hear. I began by expressing to her that what I was about to share with her was extremely painful and that I in no way blamed her or believed any of it was her fault. I began to tell her of the abuse which had taken place so many years ago. I did not express any explicit details, only that sexual abuse had taken place and that I had kept the pain of what had happened bottled up for so long that it was killing me on the inside. It was time for me to be honest with myself and those around me. I watched as a horrified expression took over my mother's face and as tears filled her eyes. She expressed deep sorrow. She had believed having a man to provide male influence in my life was the right thing for me as a young boy. She did not know what my abuser was doing and I assured her that it was not her fault. The only question she asked is if I knew where my abuser was at this time. I knew he had passed away from cancer a few years before, so I told her he was dead. She stated that it was good, because otherwise she would want to kill him. After I had finished our conversation, I called my sister and handed the phone to my mother so they could talk. I left the room. As is the case in my family, the real honest and deep issues of life are rarely discussed. For a few months, not a word was mentioned about the abuse, and there was seemingly no desire to understand what happened or its effect on my life.

It was after I had remarried and my mother was preparing to move to the area of the state where my sister lives, that she told me what when I admitted the abuse, the news "ruined her life". I realized then that the love she had for me was one of providing, of fulfilling an obligation, but not on an emotional level. She had never and could never empathize with me as her son and the ability to connect with her on a deeper level was lost. It was at this point that the confusion cleared away and anger toward my mother became a true reality. All the good intentions aside, she had let this happen to me. She even let me move out with him. As an adult looking back, this is not what a mother does to her child. The anger drove an emotional wedge between us which was unfortunately never reconciled before her death.

All that being said, it seemed to me that the more I spoke about what happened in the past, the easier it became. I shared my story with a pastor friend of mine, the same friend who took me away to clear my head a few years earlier. He knew my past had been difficult but he did not know any details. I had taken time to write out a narrative of what my childhood was like. It was only a few pages long and it proved to be very therapeutic to honestly express what happened and what I felt. I read to him what I wrote and I listened as my friend cried for me on the phone. Would that all men had a brother in Christ, a Joe, in their lives.

To this point, I had told four people who had all been very receptive and loving to me. Each had expressed their hurt for me in a different way but each had accepted what I had to say and had attempted to understand and affirm who I am as a man. I chose next to attempt to share my story with my ex-wife. I felt it was only fair to try to explain why things had been the way they were, and for her to understand how this had contributed to the downfall of our marriage. I remember standing on the driveway of my house as she was standing beside her car while I attempted to share with her the most painful events of my life. As I began to share that my past had been difficult and that I knew it contributed to the difficulties in our marriage, she quickly responded to me that I had said little things over the years and that she knew I had been abused. Her statement was bluntly, "What do you want me to do about it now?" I can honestly say, if she had been the first person I told, she would have been the only person I would have ever told. I felt as if someone had kicked me in the gut! I felt rejected and my feelings invalidated. Our marriage was over and this was simply one more piece of evidence of her inability to connect emotionally with me. Months later, she stated to me that she knew attempting to work through my past was good for me. She said she was glad I was doing it and that there were a lot of things she did not know or understand. Because I had felt so hurt by her response, I knew that I would never share or try to share those things with her again so she would never know the full story.

Telling my children was a whole other issue. I told my nineteen-year-old son first. He had heard me talk about the drinking and the fights on several occasions, but the sexual abuse had been my dark secret all my life. As I shared this with him, I could tell he was hurting. His eyes teared up and he hurt for me. But as a young man, I could tell for the next few weeks that he struggled with what I told him, so we did not talk about it anymore. Following this, my son moved some distance away and began a new life. For a time, he disconnected from myself and his mother completely. He did not want the pain of past memories to color his future. I am happy to say that now we have a very deep and meaningful relationship. I am proud of him and the man he has become. My daughter is older but since she was away at school, I waited until she came home for a weekend. I used my journaling to share my story with her. I simply read what I had written and let my rambling words speak for themselves. She cried with deep pain as I shared my story. She hugged me and said she loved me. I reflected after talking to her that she hugged me. She and Stephanie were the only ones to physically touch me or hug me when I told my story. I have no doubt some who were told on the phone would have if they had been able, but no one whom I told in person showed any physical affection other than these two. I have since come to realize how important physical affection is for victims of abuse. I had always longed for it, but had rarely received any physical affirmation in my life. My abuser was the first person who ever showed me physical affection on a regular basis. This is one of the reasons I so quickly and easily fell into his trap. The challenge is to feel safe in allowing someone to connect with you on more than a surface level, and generally any type of physical affection is reserved for relationships which move beyond the surface level. Thus, there is a dilemma, to have a yearning for something missing in your life while avoiding what would naturally allow for what was missing.

I want to emphasize once more that for a child to grow up in a dysfunctional home has long lasting effects on the adult they will become. For my mother, it was the inability to sense what was wrong in my relationship with my abuser. For my first wife, it was the inability to connect emotionally with another human being. It saddens me to say that this was passed on to my daughter. Fortunately, my son and I are close today after a time apart. We had always been close. We spent hours hunting, fishing, and camping together. Because my mother saw no value in men, and his mother's mentality was that girls were of more value than boys, my son was often targeted for criticism. During the years my mother lived with my family, this was compounded. The two of us hung together and in a sense protected each other. Because the atmosphere and the women in my son's life valued girls over boys and being outnumbered, when he was unleashed upon, I would come to his defense. My son has become a strong man with a desire to provide for his family and be a good father to his son. On the other hand, after I told my daughter, even though she expressed empathy at the moment, she has chosen to disconnect from my life. For some, everything is and will always be my fault. I share this with you to help you understand that not everyone who hears the story of abuse knows how to handle it. There will be those who for various reasons choose to disconnect from the life of the one who was abused. I always protected my children from others and, like my mother, gave them everything they needed or wanted. Looking back, I was not emotionally present in the way I should have been for my daughter which I know contributed to her critical nature of me and the inability to have a relationship with me now. The abuse I suffered as a child has reaped many consequences in my adult life. Some are able to be mended over time and I pray someday the damage done in my relationship with my daughter can be healed.

The journey to honesty has been challenging. There have been instances where truth would strike me square between the eyes. A statement or a thought which would connect several issues together, like the pieces in a puzzle. Then, it would be like the flood gates were opened as realizations and emotions came flooding into my heart and soul. Each time I have had a moment like this, I have grown in my understanding of the struggles I have had for my entire life. I know I will spend the rest of my life learning and discovering who I am and seeking to understand and incorporate my past hurts into a normal life, if there ever really is such a thing as normal.

One of the goals I have set for myself is to seek to fully understand what my past has meant for the way I have related to people around me, and with this understanding, seek to change and move deeper in my relationships. The journey which began a few years ago has led me to understand that the effects of the abuse stemming from my childhood have been far reaching. I have come to realize that the shame and guilt I carried and the fear of my heart becoming vulnerable are issues which have hindered me from entering into meaningful relationships with other people and have even caused me to stand distant in my relationship with God.

Chapter Seventeen

Guilt and Shame

One of the interesting dynamics of abuse is that it does not matter how old you are, when you think of the abuse, you still relate to it based on the age you were when it took place and to a certain extent, you get "stuck" in that time frame. I was ten years old when my abuser came into my life. I have always related to those years as that ten-year-old. The challenge is that at ten years old, I did not understand that what was happening was actually abuse. The drinking lowered my inhibitions and left me a willing participant. Because of this, all my life I have never looked at myself as someone who was abused. I believed since I was a willing participant that I was partly to blame for all the things which happened to me. The guilt and shame associated with all the immoral things which I did left me feeling I was not only to blame but in some way perverted and way beyond the realm of being normal. I lived with a conflicted heart all of my teen age years and throughout my young adult life. The struggle to understand what normal is, and what it means to live a normal life always seemed to elude my grasp. Deep inside my heart, I was ashamed of who I was and this carried over into how I lived out my relationships with others.

Shame is an emotion which will beat a person down. It kills on the inside and leaves a person scared and alone. Shame will also make a person feel like everyone else is above and beyond them. Everyone is of greater character and of higher standards than the person filled with shame. The fear which fills a heart is the fear that somehow others will find out the truth of your life and when they do you will be immediately rejected. So, the end result is that you hide! You hide the truth of your past and the struggles you live with in the present.

This was certainly the case in my life. I hid the past for more than thirty years and only now am I discovering I can be honest with the past and deal honestly with my struggles and that I don't have to fear what people think. What I understand now, as I look back at my past, is that it took a great deal of encouragement from people who love me for me to be able to accept that the ten-year-old was not responsible in any way for what happened.

This has been a major shift in thinking for myself and has allowed me to step back from the emotions of the abuse and objectively examine what happened to me from the perspective of an adult. It has allowed me to accept the reality of the abuse and understand the guilt belongs to my abuser and not myself. Accepting this reality has allowed me to begin the process of healing the deep hurts which have been present in my life since childhood. While I have proclaimed forgiveness and acceptance to others, I lived with the shame and guilt of the past and felt totally unworthy to be accepted. This false belief caused me to live a life of service for God

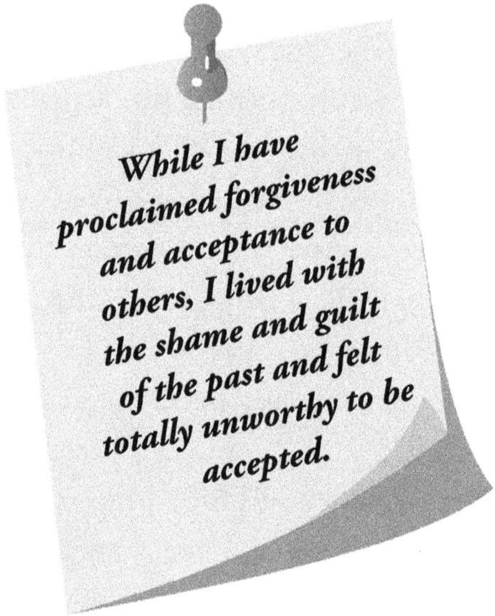

while believing myself to be distant from Him and not truly accepted by Him.

With the new understanding of guilt on the part of my abuser and not myself, I am now learning the shame I have lived with for so many years is not valid and therefore it is acceptable to let it go and live a life free from shame. The guilt which consumed my soul has been replaced by a new sense of freedom in knowing that I was not responsible and therefore none of the guilt was mine to bear.

Chapter Eighteen

Unworthiness Before God and Others

There are few things in the life of a young boy which build him up on the inside like the affirmation of his father.

There are few things in the life of a young boy which build him up on the inside like the affirmation of his father. Having grown up without a father, I was extremely eager to have this in my life. When my abuser assumed the role of father in my life, he did what no one had done before, he affirmed me as a young boy. This created a deep connection and desire in my heart to love him and do what would make him happy. When the abuse started, and as it progressed, I became very conflicted in my feelings for him. There was love and hate, and an overwhelming sense of disappointment with him and with myself. When I grew older, and began to resist him and the violence ensued; I was made to feel like a failure as a son. I had looked to him as one who would affirm me and he ended up expressing to me how much of a failure I would be, beginning with the choices of the girls I would date. As the only male figure in my life I yearned for his affirmation. When the affirmation was withheld, and I was rejected, I truly believed myself to be a failure and thus unworthy of anyone's acceptance.

The consequences of this were manifested in my life from that time forward to the present. When individuals did seek to affirm me as a young man or later in life when serving as a young pastor, I found it difficult to accept what was said as being true. I was unworthy and regardless of what was said by others, I never felt worthy or of value to anyone, especially God.

I have already expressed this earlier, but I have lived the majority of my life with the belief that God loves everyone and that Jesus died for everyone and all can go to heaven through simple faith, except me. It is not that I doubted God's love, I simply lived with the belief that of all the people of the world, I was unworthy to be loved and accepted by God.

This self-deception was based on the emotional responses to the abuse which were experienced by a boy between the ages of ten and sixteen. One of the prevalent reasons for the feelings of unworthiness is that from the ages of ten through thirteen I didn't know to resist. As I got older, I knew better, and I still didn't resist. Therefore, I was responsible for what happened. I felt guilty and unworthy for most of my life. The feeling of responsibility and my lack of resistance formulated a sense of unworthiness which left me feeling inferior to everyone around me.

Chapter Nineteen

Performance Based Identity

The ensuing years of my life found me striving to succeed in every area of my life as a way to seek approval and be accepted by others. This always meant hiding or burying my feelings down deep and attempting to be what everyone else expected me to be. There was always more which could be done and certainly more I needed to do in order to keep up the appearances and make others happy. If I didn't do this or if for some reason someone became angry or disappointed with me, it would consume me. I needed everyone to voice approval. I needed to be affirmed in order to avoid the reality of what I truly felt, which was guilt, shame, and unworthiness.

This drive to perform manifested itself in my personality as a type "A" workaholic. Now don't get me wrong, I did take time off to goof off, but I did not do vacations very well and when, on rare occasions I did, I usually took the computer to be able to work while I was away from home. I was always planning and organizing for the next event or program—always using the busyness of my activities to keep people impressed and at a distance. I was visibly too busy to bother! This lifestyle enabled me to receive affirmation through my performance while never having to delve deeper than the surface in any relationship.

The few individuals who were somewhat close to me quickly came to realize that I was very unhappy and in many ways lost emotionally. One of the challenges, which I did not accomplish very well, was to be involved with my kid's lives as they were growing up while performing for everyone else. I made most of the ball games and school performances, but looking back I could have done so much more. On the average day, the duties placed upon me and those I placed upon myself as a pastor were more than enough to create a sixty-hour plus work week. There was never a full day off and as I said, never time to truly take a vacation.

Another factor which added to this difficult situation was the fact that my marriage had been one in which we were like two friends who lived together. The emotional connection which I had longed for was absent and my heart was left yearning for what it could neither give or receive. I had closed my own heart to any real deep meaningful connection with others. There were times when instead of voicing support or giving words of encouragement, I received sharp jabs of criticism which only caused me to pull further away to protect my heart from harm. This also served to affirm my sense of unworthiness both in earthly relationship as well as my relationship with God.

Chapter Twenty

A Closed Heart

One of the things that I have touched on previously is one of the most important. When I was ten, I was yearning for a man to show me some attention. Having never had a father, I was excited to have a man give me attention and because of this, I truly came to love him deeply. My heart was filled with excitement as each new day and opportunity came my way in this new relationship. When the abuse actually began the love which was present was mixed with pain and confusion. The longer the abuse continued, the more the love was replaced with anger and ultimately self-hatred.

In attempting to describe what I now understand more clearly, I have searched my heart and mind for an image which would make sense. The one which works for me is that of a multi-leveled heart with both an elevator and stairway. When I was ten, a man entered the elevator. It descended very quickly to a depth in my heart which no one had ever reached. It descended quickly until the abuse started. The elevator then abruptly stopped, but the descent did not. The tightly winding staircase was used. The relationship was still growing deeper during the time of confusion but at a much slower pace. When the anger and self-hatred set into my heart, I began to pull away from the relationship and suffer the consequences. What all this accomplished in my life was for me to close my heart to allowing anyone to ever reach the depths he had reached. True, deep, connecting love was associated with pain and hurt. It was therefore necessary to seal the deepest portions of my heart and keep everyone on a more superficial level. I have described this as allowing people to reach a certain depth of love or caring and then to be blocked from going any deeper by a bolted steel door. The most intimate, deepest parts of my heart were sealed and no one was allowed to enter. To love at such a depth was to chance being hurt and I was not willing to risk it.

This is the way I lived in every relationship. I was able to love but only with a superficial love which always left me wanting more but always scared to allow anyone to go deep enough to give me what I was truly yearning to receive. The result of this in my life has been that everyone who would have wanted to grow closer to me has been kept at a distance so that I might be assured that my heart was protected. I am sure the deepest places in my heart would have remained sealed if it were not for the love and acceptance of one individual. With this one person, I shared a common experience of hurt and pain, and the fear of allowing others to know what suffering had been endured. For whatever reason, Stephanie was able to move beyond the steel door to reach a depth of love and trust which I had not allowed in over thirty years. Because of the common sense of experience, I was able to take the risk and trust someone enough to share my secret. On that dirt road in the middle of nowhere, I cried and talked, and talked and cried and I was accepted and affirmed. The experience of that one moment revealed to me that it was possible to open my heart and not be hurt. While it is still a risk, I have been shown that it is possible to trust and love and that even though hurts might come my way, the reward of true loving relationships are worth the risk. She also revealed a true picture of the grace of God. Even in our most volatile and undeserving moments, He is waiting for us with open arms and unconditional love.

This understanding of unconditional love is what I had been unable to grasp throughout my adult life. Stephanie is a woman who loves God and who lives each day with a heart which is open to loving and accepting others. Her love for God and her absolute love of Jesus is clearly seen by everyone who knows her. The Apostle Paul wrote, *Do you not know that you are God's temple and that God's Spirit dwells in you?* (1 Corinthians 3:16 ESV). It was in that moment on the dirt road that her heart was united with God's heart to reveal to me that I could be worthy of true love. True love from another human being and true love from God.

Chapter Twenty-One

Discovering the Reality of Love

The reality of what love is supposed to be as opposed to what I experienced in my life is something which has taken a great deal of time and discernment to understand. As a pastor, I have often taught the meaning of true love. I have parsed the Greek words and studied the texts in order to relay to others the different types of love we experience in life and the proper role of each. What I realize now is that for myself, it was all only academic.

What is love supposed to be? The Bible says that God is love! He is a God who loves unconditionally. He is a God who loves fully and completely. He is *Father*. For many years, this image of God presented a challenge for me because the only father figure I ever had in my life was someone I loved but who caused me great pain. Because of this, God as Father was not a very comforting image. It was only after my own children were born and my parental desire to protect my children from any harm and danger came to fully bear on my life that my view of God as Father began to change. To be a parent, to be entrusted with the life of another individual to care for and protect caused me to reflect on my own past and to seek to take the good and leave the bad behind and apply what was positive to my children. While I was able to do this in my expression of love for my children, I was not able to allow others,

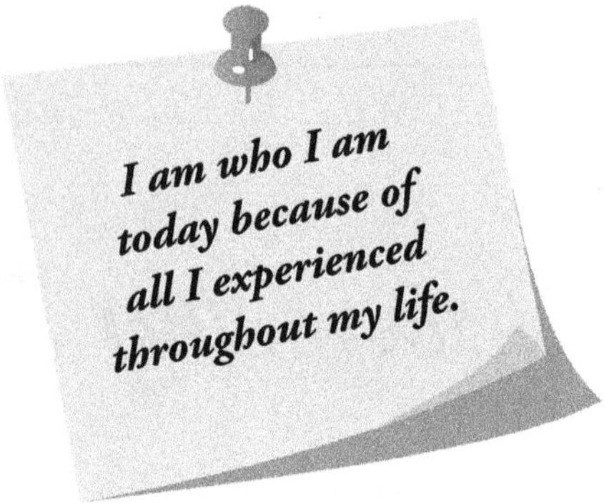

not even my children, to do this for me. Even those whom I loved dearly were kept at least some distance away and never allowed to enter the deepest recesses of my heart, lest my secret be discovered.

As I have learned to reflect on God as Father being a positive image, I have slowly learned what it means to accept the love of a father. If I might step out on a limb and be a little preachy for a moment, God is a Father who loves us as His children! What I experienced and possibly what you experienced as a child is not what God wanted for us. He did not want me to suffer abuse. I now understand that the heart of God was hurting with me and for me when I suffered. He was there with me, walking each step of the way and supporting me when I did not know what to do! When I sat with a gun in my hand ready to end my life, I have no doubt God kept me from going through with it because He had something greater in store for me. When I left home and stayed gone for more than a year, He enabled me to find a place where I could be safe and heal for a time. When I needed to run a second time, God was faithful to lead me in a way I am only now beginning to see and understand. What I know is this, true love does anything and everything necessary to bless the one who is loved. God has certainly shown us His desire to do this for each of us. I realize that as soon as I say this there will be some who will say that God does not love me because if He did, He would have intervened and stopped the abuse from happening. It is true that God is God and He can do anything He wants to do. Could He have intervened and stopped my abuse even before it started? *Yes.* Could He have rescued me out of it at any point during the five years it was happening? *Yes.* Does the fact that He did not intervene in a miraculous way mean He is not a God of love? *No.* God's love is seen in that He is able to sustain us and give us strength to endure what we face in this life. We are able to learn from it and allow Him to use it to accomplish something meaningful to bless another person's life. I am who I am today because of all I experienced throughout my life. Take away any single event and I would be changed forever. This is even true of the abuse I suffered. It was as I began to understand that God had not abandoned me, but that He in fact had been loving me all my life that I began to honestly look at what it means when God says He loves me.

When God created Adam and placed him in the garden, it was never His intent that Adam live alone. He was created in the image of God, and as such he was created for the purpose of living in relationship with others, even as God; Father, Son, and Holy Spirit exists in relationship. Adam was to live in relationship with God, but also in relationship with other people, namely Eve. Eve was created to be one with Adam and their relationship was to be a reflection of the intimacy and love which God had with them and for them. One of the most meaningful passages of Scripture for me personally is Genesis 3:10, *God came walking in the garden in the cool of the day.* The image is that God came walking in the garden in the cool of the day, every day. He came to the garden, manifesting Himself in some visible way which allowed Him to *walk* in the garden. He came in a human form to walk with the man and woman He created. He came to live in a relationship with them, even as they lived each day in a re-

> ***What I know is this, true love does anything and everything necessary to bless the one who is loved.***

lationship with each other. The relationship between God and man was destroyed when Adam and Eve ate of the tree. The relationship between Adam and Eve was destroyed at the same time. The damage done by sin could only be undone and healed by absolute true love. The entire message of the Bible and in fact all human history from the fall in the garden to this very moment in time reveals all God has done to heal each of us with His love. There was nothing, no limit and no boundary to the love God has or the sacrifice He would make to love His children. From the garden to the cross, from the cross to today, everything has been directed by God so each of us would hear once more of His love for us and how special we are to Him, each of us individually and personally.

God has revealed that it is in His heart to protect and save us because He loves us.

God has revealed that it is in His heart to protect and save us because He loves us. When our hearts become closed to love because of the pain we experience and fear enters into our hearts as a result, we begin to have a warped image of God. We see Him as distant and uncaring. We believe He loves others more than us, if He loves us at all. The result of this warped view of God is that we lock God out of our heart, just as if we close the doors and bolt them tight, not allowing people to enter either. This is certainly what I did throughout my life. God is a God of love! I preached it, taught it, even believed it, but always in relation to others and never for myself. It was only when I took the risk to trust and share my secret with a person who did not reject, but affirmed me that I began to understand love. It is amazing to me now, as I look back, to see how God was working through one person to show me what was in His heart. His desire for all the years I was hiding was to help me open my heart and experience His love and the love of others. I was the one who was unwilling to take the chance. But when the time was right, God sent the one person He was able to use to accomplish His will in my life.

Chapter Twenty-Two

Discovering the Reality of Forgiveness

I would like to take a moment to speak about my journey toward forgiveness. Not my forgiveness! I am eternally grateful that I can now proclaim boldly that I am forgiven of all my sins through the blood Jesus shed for me. When Jesus went to the cross, it was for me just as much as it was for everyone else. Forgiveness is real and forgiveness is freeing. When the moment came and I fully understood that I could stand guiltless, with no shame, before my God and other people, it was the moment I was set free. Free from the self-inflicted guilt and shame for the past as well as celebrating true forgiveness for the real sins I was guilty of in my life. We know and confess God's forgiveness is free. We are, however, often unwilling to give this free forgiveness to others.

Over the years as I have walked this journey of healing, I can honestly say that the idea of forgiving my abuser has been difficult. The relationship with my mother is a whole other story. There was one occasion when I was still very young that my abuser took me on a trip to visit his childhood home. He was born and raised in Hattiesburg, Mississippi, and for a young boy from Texas this was a whole other world. We traveled through the backwood swamps to visit some of his relatives. I remember being horrified by the run-down shacks people lived in. The dingy, humid surroundings and the dense swamp-land forests were a sight. We pulled up one day to a house where his uncle lived. His uncle was sitting in a chair on the porch of his shack. He was wearing nothing but a ratty old dirty t-shirt and underwear, just sitting on the porch drinking beer. Of course, we sat on the porch and drank a beer with him. My memories of that trip and the places we visited have helped me understand the upbringing my abuser experienced was less than desirable. I mentioned earlier that my abuser had contracted cancer and died. What I did not share is that he had returned to Hattiesburg before his death and is buried there. I have often found myself daydreaming about traveling to the deep South to find his grave. I assure you it is not for sentimental reasons. For many years, I have simply wanted to stand and piss on his grave. What I have come to realize is that I was wanting to exact some revenge on my abuser! But what would that get me! Would I feel any better? Would it make the hurt and heartache of the years of abuse all go away? Even if my abuser were still alive and willing to apologize for all he had done to me, would that make a difference in the journey of my life or the struggles I have faced over the years?

I needed to journey the road of forgiveness to truly be released from the hold he had in my life.

I finally realized there is absolutely nothing which he could ever do, or suffer, which could truly make a difference in my life. I have lived for many years desiring to "exact my pound of flesh" only to arrive at the understanding that even if I could accomplish this, it would not make any difference. I needed to journey the road of forgiveness to truly be released from the hold he had in my life.

There is much confusion when people hear the word forgiveness. To many, the idea of forgiving is equated with excusing. Thus, to forgive an abuser is to proclaim that what that person did to me or to you was okay or justified. This is not what forgiveness means and it is something I could never and would never do. To other people, the idea of forgiveness is one of simply forgetting the past offense and pretending it never happened. Again, I can't do this, nor would I want to. What happened to me was real and it was wrong. It cannot be excused or forgotten! In fact, just the opposite. My story as well as every other abuse story needs to be told and the abusers in our midst need to be held accountable for their actions.

Forgiveness is not about the actions of the abuser. What my abuser did was heinous and the pain inflicted into my life alone was at one point almost unbearable, not to mention how many other lives were touched and affected by the pain he inflicted. As I said, forgiveness is not about my abuser but in reality it is about me. I was the one carrying the pain and I was the one desiring revenge, which in reality could not bring healing into my heart. Forgiveness is not about getting even, but best understood as canceling a debt. I felt like my abuser owed me something, which if I could get from him, would make my pain subside. Standing here today I can assure you there is nothing my abuser could ever do which could make up for the pain he brought into my life.

I seriously doubt that before my abuser died he ever even once considered what he did to me inflicted pain or had any lasting, long term negative consequences. Guilt was not part of his vocabulary and he was in reality beyond any concern for anyone but himself, which is true for every abuser. What I had to wrestle with was the reality that I was the one who was burdened down by the experiences, not him. I was the one who needed to deal with my feelings and emotions, not him. He didn't care, but it was killing me.

It was a choice on the part of God to forgive so His own heart was set free to love.

Forgiveness is not about justifying, excusing, or forgetting what happened in the past. Forgiving is about setting your own heart free to move forward into the rest of your life. Forgiveness is about letting go of the need to take control of the past hurt and placing it into God's hands, trusting that He will do what is right and I can trust Him to make the right decision according to His will and justice. God does not make mistakes. He will do what is right concerning my abuser and because I know God is good and that He loves me, I am free to let go of my desire for revenge and trust Him with the pain I have carried for so many years. I also feel I need to clarify an often-misunderstood fact about forgiveness. Forgiveness is not a feeling or emotion. Forgiveness is a choice! Generally speaking it does not feel good to give forgiveness to a person who has hurt you. There is a part of me which despises the idea of forgiving the man who abused me, especially since he never even apologized for the pain I have suffered at those hands. When I finally came to the point that the weight bearing down on my own heart was more than I could bear, I knew it was time to begin to let it go and give it to God. It was a choice, not a feeling. To put forgiveness into perspective, please know it did not feel good for God to forgive me or anyone in this world. It meant a painful choice to do what was right even when everything screamed for the opposite. Envision Jesus hanging on the cross, suffering for the sins of the whole world when He was totally innocent. There was nothing in those actions which brought any good feelings. It was a choice on the part of God to forgive so His own heart was set free to love. Holding on to unforgiveness was a burden my heart carried for years, which was part of the reason I was unable to love or be loved to the fullest extent. The choice to forgive has removed the burden and opened the way for love to become a reality in my life.

Now please understand what I am saying! There is a great difference between God's eternal justice and human justice. If my abuser were still alive, I truly believe it would be right and proper to attempt to prosecute him to the fullest extent of the law. What he did was a crime by any standard and there should be human consequences for his actions. Holding an individual accountable for their actions is a totally different issue than forgiveness. Accountability is about the law and justice demanded for a criminal act. Forgiveness is about my heart and the burden I carried for years.

Possibly a simple illustration can be useful! If a man robs a bank, should he be punished to the fullest extent of the law? The answer is obviously yes. Can this same man be forgiven for robbing the bank? Again, the answer is yes. If the man is forgiven, do they open the jail cell and set him free? No! He must pay his debt to society and only after that debt is paid can he be set free. Yet, the moment this individual truly repents and asks for forgiveness for his crime, God does forgive him. He can be set free in his spirit and know he is loved by God while serving his time in prison. When we choose to forgive, we are making a choice to let go of our need and demand for personal justice and we are allowing God to be God.

I would like to be able to tell you that I have been able to fully and completely forgive my abuser. Sadly, I cannot! I will say that it is a back and forth struggle in my life. There may come a day when I have fully let the anger go and the struggle will finally be over. Most likely I will continue having to make the choice to forgive and say it hundreds of more times in the future as I have in the past. It is a choice I made which I am seeking to live into. I have grown through the events of my life to the point that I rarely think of my abuser. When I do, I often find myself wondering what happened to him as a child which warped him into the man he became. The love/hate feelings still exist in my own heart for the man who was my father/abuser. But honesty demands me to also tell you that on the days when I feel burdened, I still feel the tinge of desiring revenge. While these feelings are fewer and farther between, they still do occur. This has helped me to understand that forgiveness is not always a single moment in time. With most people and in most situations I can do this. But in the case of my abuser and because of the deep lasting pain he inflicted in my life, I have to admit that forgiveness is more like a journey than a single moment. The difference is that I now understand that forgiveness for my abuser is not about him but about me. Because of this, I want to grow to the point that I can fully and finally forgive so that my own heart can be completely free from the power the past had over me. It truly is a journey and a goal I work towards always.

The feelings I have struggled with in regard to my abuser are vastly different than that of my relationship with my mother. As a young teenager, I did not blame my mother for what happened to me. I felt she was blindly innocent to the events which were happening. As an adult, looking back, I can see how many times she failed me as my mother. I'm not saying that any parent is perfect. We all fail but even with this, I never felt that she was responsible for what happened. This changed after I shared with her my story of abuse. Her response that I had *ruined her life* has brought forth different and more difficult issues to discuss. Those words spoken from her concerning all the things I endured because of her failure as a mother were in some ways more painful than the abuse itself. That moment was a reality check for me. I stated earlier that I did not believe she had it in her, because of her past, to truly connect with me or anyone on an emotional level. The statement she made to me was not about how the abuse affected my life! It was about how it made her feel! It was not about love for me, but about her love for herself and how I had pushed deeper emotionally than she was willing or able to go. So what about forgiveness? As I said, I never really blamed her. All the years I suffered in silence I just felt sorry for her. As difficult as it may seem to you as you read this, I did not really want to tell her about my abuse because I knew it would be painful for her to hear. I told her of my abuse because it was needful for my own heart to be honest with everyone in my life. The fallout of her statement to me about ruining her life was that my blood ran cold. I felt no desire to blame her or hold her accountable. I wanted no revenge or payment of any kind. I did not want anything, including any type of relationship. After she moved to the other side of the state, I saw her only once before she passed away. It was a short trip to visit her when she was well beyond the ability to communicate in any way. It was a final visit motivated by duty and a simple sense that it was the right thing to do. It was also needful to do this with my son who needed that one final visit before she was gone. The resulting emotions I have felt since the moment those words were spoken have been of emptiness and loss. When my biological father died, I grieved the loss of the idea of a father. When my mother spoke those words my hope for a real true relationship with her died. I grieved the loss of having a mother long before she took her final breath in this world. Looking back after the years have passed, I see the truth of the generational curse of abuse in all its

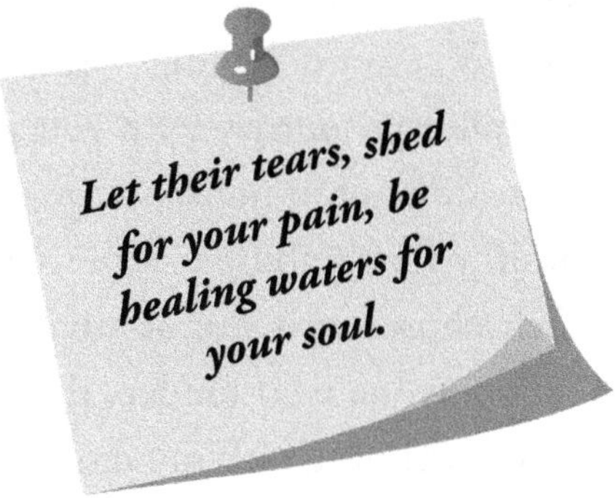

forms as it creates heartache and hardship on all who are touched by it.

Having said all the previous concerning my struggles with my mother and our relationship, I know there will be some who read this who truly do struggle with anger toward a parent(s) who failed them as a child. It is the duty of a parent to nurture and protect a child as they grow to adulthood. When a parent fails to provide this protection and abuse becomes part of a child's life, it is normal and natural to blame the parent(s) involved. This will affect every aspect of your relationship with your family. When your family gathers for Christmas dinners the event is stilted, and birthdays lack a certain celebration. If your parent(s) is receptive to talking about your abuse then do so. Sometimes, when you simply experience the hurt and heartache they feel as you share your story it can help in your healing and open the way for the process of forgiveness to begin. Let them hurt for you. Let their tears, shed for your pain, be healing waters for your soul. But please remember, forgiveness is not about them but about you. Forgiveness is about setting your heart free to be who God has created you to be and become. The unwillingness to forgive will prolong your healing and in truth it will set up a barrier to true healing which you will never be able to cross until forgiveness takes place in your heart.

There is a reality I have yet to speak about thus far in this story. There are people who will be supportive and who will help you on your journey toward healing. There are also people who are truly unable to walk this journey with you and who will in fact make your journey more difficult, if not sabotage it all together. In the same way, it is unhealthy for an abuse victim to ever be around or have any contact with their abuser, it is just as advisable for a victim of abuse to disconnect from anyone who hinders them on their healing journey. For myself, this disconnect with my mother was made easier due to distance, but it was necessary. Anyone who minimizes the abuse or redirects the consequences of abuse is not a person to be trusted with your heart. This is a person who will hurt you again in the future. Forgiveness was not really an issue in the emotions I felt for my mother. For myself, it was sadness. The relationship was over even before her death made it final. The challenge I faced at that moment was the aloneness I felt at having no parent left in this world due to these odd circumstances. What I had already learned was that I had the support I needed in my wife and children who drew close to me and helped me through those difficult days.

I am sure among the majority of abuse victims my story is unique. For most parents who find out their child has been sexually abused, there is a deep sense of failure mixed with pain and anger. For most parents who must face their own failures in parenting, there is a desire to support the abuse victim on their journey of healing. When a parent is honest and admits their failure in protecting their child the way is opened for a new and different relationship to begin. Trust can be established and the future can become vastly different than what was experienced in the past. When the adult survivor does struggle with anger and unforgiveness toward a parent(s) the need for forgiveness is just a valid as for the abuser. The difference is that while forgiveness for the abuser is needed, there can never be any type of relationship, ever! With a parent who failed to protect a child from abuse, forgiveness can open the way to build a healthy and mutually supportive relationship which never existed in the past.

While some people find it within themselves to forgive others who failed them, I can personally assure you that for myself this was made easier as I grew to understand the forgiveness I received in my life. If each of us can objectively set aside the abuse we suffered for just a moment and think about or own lives and the mistakes we have made of which we are personally responsible, we must all confess we have blown it. I am a sinful human being. That has nothing to do with my abuse or my abuser. I am personally deserving of judgment because I am personally guilty of sinning against a holy God. The wonderful truth is that even when I was guilty and deserving of nothing good, God chose to give me everything. The following verse of Scripture resonated in my heart the first time I read it years ago:

> *He has delivered us from the domain of darkness and transferred us to the kingdom of his beloved Son, in whom we have redemption, the forgiveness of sins.* **Colossians 1:13-14**

It literally means God reached down out of heaven, picked me up, rescuing me from Satan's dominion and God then set me down in the kingdom of His Son. All this happened in the instant I received the forgiveness of my sins through His grace. The verse says, "we have redemption" which means Jesus redeemed us or paid the price for us. For an abuse survivor to truly grasp the full extent of God's love in Jesus, changes everything. It declares their absolute worth and value to God, that He would pay the price to rescue them. It is when a survivor truly believes he/she has worth and value simply because of who they are as an individual human being the way is opened up for healing to begin. When the shame and guilt are washed away and a person can truly believe God celebrates who they are as His child, then the way is opened to trust God as we begin the process of forgiving others.

Chapter Twenty-Three

Abuser or Protector?

One of the things I can honestly say I learned about myself early on, which has enabled me to serve in an effective way as a pastor, is that the abuse I suffered as a child created in me the desire to help other people in a desperate way. Throughout my years of serving as a pastor, I was drawn to those situations where an individual was hurting and I came with a desire to help bring the hurting to an end. This was evidenced by the number of hours I would spend with hospice patients and their families, the hours spent counseling individuals and couples, and especially when I discovered someone was in an abusive relationship. There has been arguably no limit to what I have been willing to do to assist a person in an abusive relationship be free from the pain and hurt the abuse was causing.

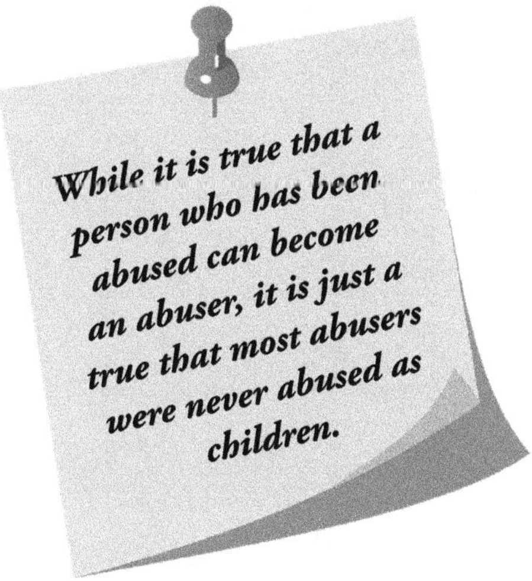

I am who I am as an adult survivor of childhood sexual abuse and I do not want to change who I am if I can make a difference in the lives of those around me. I realize there are many books on the topic of abuse which quote statistics concerning how many children who are abused will grow up to become abusers. While it is true that a person who has been abused can become an abuser, it is just as true that most abusers were never abused as children. What is just as true is the fact that many survivors of abuse become avid protectors of those who are hurting and do not have the strength to help themselves. It is truly one of the ways that God works in a horrible situation to mold us and shape us to be used by Him to accomplish good in the world. There have been many opportunities where I have reflected on the reality that I am a protector and I have even wondered if I would be such a protector if I had not suffered the abuse I did as a child. While I would love to be able to roll back the hands of time and undo the abuse I suffered, I would not want to be someone different than I am today. I want to be the protector who stands up for and alongside those who are suffering. I want to give support to those who need it and enable them to find the strength to free themselves from abusive situations and encourage them each step they take toward new freedom and independence. I am who I am as an adult survivor of childhood sexual abuse and I do not want to change who I am if I can make a difference in the lives of those around me.

Chapter Twenty - Four

The Journey to Freedom and Life

As I sit to write this closing section of my story, I want to tell you of the wonderful journey and the life changing transformations which have taken place in my life. I share this with you because our God is a God of hope who uses individual lives to reveal not only what He is capable of accomplishing but what His heart desires to accomplish for each of His children.

Stephanie, the woman I love and our wedding day picture.

I wrote earlier that Stephanie is the woman who sat with me on a dirt road, the first person I ever told my secret to, and I celebrate every day that she is now my wife. She has been the most influential person in my life! Not only is she beautiful on the inside as well as the outside, but she has captured my heart in a way I never knew was possible. She is a godly lady who has grown to become the wife of a pastor who everyone in the congregation truly loves. She works hard in the church, side by side with me, and she truly has a heart for the work of God in the church. She is a dynamic prayer warrior who not only lifts me up in prayer but who also looks beyond our own needs to prayer for so many more people than I have ever taken the time to pray for in the past. We pray together! This was an absolutely new thing for me. I was always the "up front" person who prayed, or the "designated" person as the pastor of the church. It was more of a job responsibility rather than a passion. She had taught me what passion for God is like by living it out before my very eyes.

She has journeyed with me these last few years and I can honestly say it has been a wonderful journey. There have been difficult moments. The transition to a new church body was long and often grueling, but Steph was always there with words of encouragement. The first appointment given to us in the Methodist church was at a small, declining, 100% African American congregation. Steph is a beautiful blond and all her kids have a fair complexion and light hair as well. We entered on the first Sunday to serve and there were eight people in attendance besides us. That's right, eight people! The congregation was on the other side of the tracks, literally! It was a part time position which meant for the first time I would have to assume a worker/priest role as a pastor. I had always served in larger parishes which were able to provide a full-time salary. The church was without a musician, so Steph was right there, playing the piano while I preached and took care of the members. We served that small black church for almost five years. It proved to be one of the most rewarding experiences in my life as a pastor. The church grew to an average attendance over fifty with a youth ministry and Bible study opportunities and a great amount of outreach into the community. We raised up a new pastor from the midst of the membership and left to serve a new appointment with the confidence that we could see how God can work when we are willing to look for Him in action. While at this small church, Steph began two different businesses. The first was a home daycare. One summer afternoon when I counted all the daycare kids and our kids who had friends visiting, I cooked lunch for seventeen kids in our home. Our home was like this continually. If it wasn't the daycare kids and parents over visiting, it was friends from school or our friends who had become like family. Even today some of the closest friends who we consider family were born of our time in that small church.

During those first years together and serving in the church, I worked as a land-man for the oil companies. I worked at a funeral home, taught school for a year, and helped Steph as much as I could. When she closed the daycare and opened a cooking business, I learned how challenging being a good chef could be. She provided home cooked meals for families whose lives were so busy they generally ate out. She did this as a ministry! She wanted to provide a whole meal for five people for less money than it would take to eat at a restaurant. Even through this, we made more new friends and many doors were opened to minister to people's lives.

I am now once again appointed to a full time pastoral position. The churches I have served in recent years have been larger with even greater potential. Some of our kids have married and others are still in school.

Our family is truly a family. We talk about everything. God's will, His love and grace, and the meaning of His Word are frequent topics in our home. We are still extremely busy but it is a good feeling to be able to serve God not only with joy but with the assurance and confidence of knowing He is present and working to bless people's lives through what we are doing.

I realized some time back that something in my own heart and soul changed. I mentioned earlier that I believed I would die young and deservedly go to hell. I stated that I was okay with this as the reality of my future. I no longer feel this way. I have grown to love life and to live life to the fullest. I know some day I will leave this world and that is normal and I accept it, but I want it to be a long time in the future. I want to love my wife and serve my God for as long as He will allow me to do so. I want to see Him work in the world, the church, and through us and I am looking for it. I am still a protector and I still find myself going to extreme lengths to help those in need, especially where abuse is present. The difference in my life now is that Steph is right there with me, every step of the way.

My preaching and ministry have changed a great deal. I believe it is more real and impactful on the lives of those who attend. Everyone in the congregation knows my story! I have no secrets past or present. I live my life as an open book. Abuse and the needs of others is a frequent topic but overarching everything is how big and great and wonderful our God is. I'm excited for the future! I want to see what is going to happen tomorrow, next week, and next year. I have found that if I simply place all my trust in God, He will be faithful today as He has been through every step of my life.

When I was a little boy riding down the highway with Brother Ramsey and he asked me what I wanted to be when I grew up, and I told him I wanted to be a preacher. Now having served as an ordained pastor for over a quarter of a century I had an older member walk out of church following the service, and he wanted to tell me something. Often people comment to me following a service that they like the sermon or it touched them in some way. One gentleman came to me with a statement that was beyond my ability to grasp at first. Ed told me he had finally figured it out. Evidently it had been puzzling him for a while. He looked me straight in the eyes and said, "I finally figured it out. You were born to be a preacher of God's Word!"

God has been faithful to me, even when I was enduring some of the darkest times in my life. His promises to me were true when I did not even know them. He formed me and knit me together in my mother's womb and called me into His service even before I was born. In times past, I did not understand this, but today I do. The very first sermon Jesus preached in the Synagogue as He began His earthly ministry was on the text of Isaiah which is recorded in Luke's Gospel:

> ***The Spirit of the Lord is upon me, because he has anointed me to proclaim good news to the poor. He has sent me to proclaim liberty to the captives and recovering of sight to the blind, to set at liberty those who are oppressed, to proclaim the year of the Lord's favor. And he rolled up the scroll and gave it back to the attendant and sat down. And the eyes of all in the synagogue were fixed on him. And he began to say to them, "Today this Scripture has been fulfilled in your hearing."*** **Luke 4:18-21**

Did you hear it? *To proclaim good news to the poor. . . proclaim liberty to the captives . . . and recovery of sight to the blind, to set at liberty those who are oppressed, to proclaim the year of the Lord's favor.* In His very first sermon, Jesus was speaking about what He had come to do for me and so many others like me. I was broken as a child and felt unworthy. I lived as an adult with deep wounds and a longing to be wanted. I believed God could and did love and want everyone, except me. But Jesus said He had come for me! To bring good news and to set me free from all which held me in bondage for all those years. To open my eyes to see the truth. The truth of the past and the truth of the present. To allow me to see the past for what it really was, abuse and the one who was guilty and that person was not me. I have been enabled to see my Father who loves me and wants me to be with Him forever. I am no longer the one who is oppressed. No longer weighted down by the burden I carried for so long in my life. Jesus has set me free to be a child of God and to know with certainty that God in heaven never takes His eyes off of me because He loves me.

So, I will live my life today differently than I lived in the past. I am on a journey from the cradle to the grave, but I'm no longer rushing to get there and I no longer believe this is what I deserve. Jesus used the love of my future wife and her acceptance of me when I told her my secret and her enduring love for me to work something new in my heart. Now don't get me wrong, God did it, but God often chooses people and works through them to touch and change lives. I will always be a work in progress, but isn't that true for all of us? God enters in with His love and grace and we change. We begin a transformation which moves us day by day to be more like our Savior. Our lives change and most importantly our hearts change and we begin to see the world through His eyes.

One day the transformation will be complete! One day my journey in this world will come to an end and I do look forward to that day. Remember, I'm not rushing to get there but I now know what that day will hold for me. I will close my eyes here and I will see Jesus with arms open wide to welcome me home! And I will see my Father, my true Father who, with a smile on His face, will not only be glad to see me but He will welcome me to the place He has always wanted me to be. I will be with God, with the one who has always loved me and been with me throughout my journey.

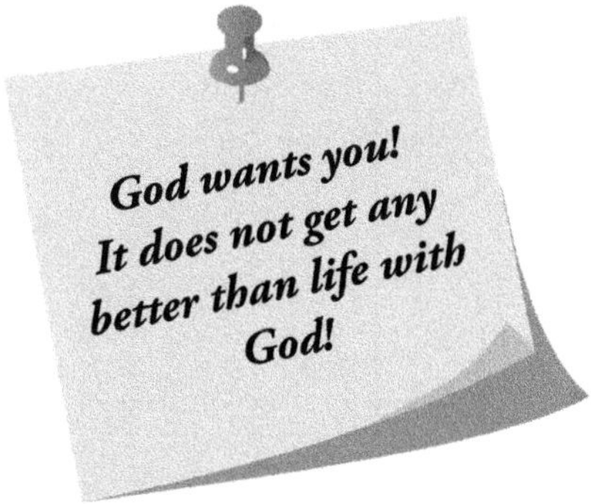

Please to not lose sight of the greatest truth revealed in God's Word. What has been true for me in my life is exactly that same truth for your life. God wants you! He has always loved you and wanted you from before time began. He is present, here for you. He will heal your wounds and transform you by the power of His love and grace. He will enable you to shift your eyes from the pain of the past to have hope for the future. He does this because it is in His heart to love you unconditionally and completely. You're on a journey, along with me, Steph, our kids, and all those you know. You are on a journey which will be the ride of your life. You're on a journey to see God work and reveal Himself to you, make you whole, and use you to touch the lives of others who need Him. You're on a journey! Enjoy the ride! It does not get any better than life with God!

Chapter Twenty - Five

Epilogue

There is a sense in which this book will never be finished. This story will continue to change and develop even as I continue to grow and become the man God desires for me to be. I am learning! I am growing and changing with each new day and each new opportunity God brings into my life. Steph and I have moved forward in many ways. She has become a champion for me and I can assure you I celebrate what God has and will continue to accomplish in her life and through her.

Having made the transition into the Methodist Church, I have had my theological horizons broadened. Not in any way changing what I have believed, but a fuller revelation, a fleshing out if you will. One of the cornerstones of what I now understand to be true is what I can now look back and see present in my life from an early age. God was there! There has never been a moment in my life when I was alone, even in the times of deep hurt or despair. In the church we call this prevenient grace, which is simply the grace which goes before us in life. It is a technical term for what we all know to be true, but which is often difficult to put into words. It is also the grace of God which we rarely understand until we look back and see what God has accomplished in our past.

Prevenient grace works like this. When I was a little boy who was missing out on the tender affection of a mother, God provided for me a grandmother who would hold me in her lap, give me hugs, and tell me that she loved me. She was an instrument in the hand of God to reveal to me real, unconditional love. When I was with Brother Ramsey in the car, speeding down the highway, answering his questions about what I wanted to be with I grew up. God was there, revealing in my young heart that He was calling me to a higher purpose in my life. He was going to use me to preach the Gospel and reveal His love to untold numbers of people as a pastor in His church. God was even working in the young couple who lived next door to me when I was a small boy, who took me to church where I learned basic truths about God in Sunday School. In all these things, God was laying a foundation which He would, in time, build upon.

Then came the days of frightening darkness. The abuse started and I was taken as far away from all the things of God as a person could be taken. As I look back, I never got angry at God or questioned why He was not present or why He did not intervene and stop the abuse. Maybe I simply didn't know enough to even ask those questions. What I now know and understand is He was there! In those deepest, darkest times, God was there with me! I did not see Him, or hear Him, although I do believe there were opportunities I missed when He could have intervened. One of those missed opportunities came when Jim, the young man next door, caught me outside and told me that I did not have to avoid he and his wife simply because I wasn't going to church with them anymore. Knowing what I know today, I realize this was a missed opportunity to have an adult intervene and rescue me. I simply failed to see or seize it at the time.

In his book, *The Shack*, the author Wm. Paul Young describes a moment when Jesus is telling of the little girl, Missy's, time of abuse. Jesus is speaking to Mac (Missy's father) when Mac lashes out because Missy was all alone with the terrible man who hurt her. Jesus listens and then assures this little child's father that she was not alone. He (Jesus) was with her through everything she endured. She was never alone. There were times I truly felt alone in the midst of the abuse I suffered. Looking back now I can see that I was not alone. God was present with me to sustain me and to bring me out the other side of those horrible situations and in the end, He desired to bless me.

I have always believed that I did not pull the trigger when I was staring down the barrel of my pistol because I did not want my mother to have to clean up the mess! But in everything I have shared, was that really the reason? There was no great amount of affection with my mother! There was certainly no bond which held us together. She had let me move out with my abuser and then move back in, only to leave and travel hundreds of miles with him without her knowing anything about what we were doing. Why did it not pull the trigger? The only real explanation I have is that God was there! He wanted me to live. He had other things, good things in store for me and He was using that crises moment to work in my life and get me away from my abuser.

There are other things I cannot explain apart from God and His grace being present throughout those difficult days. I assure you that I have not exaggerated concerning the amount and abuse of alcohol.

There are very few types of alcohol we did not drink and in great quantity. When I stated earlier that I do not remember very much about my junior high years, I was telling the truth. I really did go to school almost every day with a hangover. I would be sick until about lunch time and by the end of the day we would start the drinking all over again. Not one single teacher questioned. There was no intervention on the part of the school. But through what was five years of massive alcohol abuse, I never became an alcoholic. Neither did I ever become addicted to the drugs which were plentiful. If that is not the grace of God, I do not know what is!

When I did run, I did not know where I was going, only that I needed to go. What are the chances of a sixteen-year-old drop out finding a place to provide a job with room and board? I never had to sleep in my truck and I never went hungry. I also was provided with a place to heal for a time. I will readily admit that the time on the horse ranch was a time when I took very little care of my body, it was a time when my heart found some measure of peace. The abuse had ended, and I was safe! For a child who has been abused, this is one of the greatest gifts of God's grace.

While I did not know what I was searching for, I see how God was searching for me.

While I did not know what or who I was searching for, I can look back now and see how God was searching for me. A simple invitation from a friend to attend a young adult Bible study group turned into a lifetime of service to God. While I did it wrong for many years, teach fervently of God's love for everyone but myself, God finally broke through into the deep dark sealed depths of my heart. He did not do it as I studied, or prepared sermons, or even while I was assuring other victims of His love for them. God broke through on a dirt road in the middle of nowhere, all in the name of love. His love for me and Steph's love for me. Was it a risk? Yes! Was I scared? Again, Yes! Did it happen? Absolutely! Because this was God's plan all along. He was there on the dirt road and every moment of my life looking back to the memories of riding in great-uncle Jim's pickup truck. He has always been present, leading me and guiding me with the desire that I could come to truly know that He loves me and desires for me to experience His love and grace.

Once the steel door on my heart was unbolted, I experienced true love. I was able to understand that another human being could accept me and love me in spite of all that I believed I was. Over the years which have followed, I have been able to accept love from other people and believe it was real and genuine. What began with Steph and has been expanded to our children and beyond to many friends who have truly become our family. At the same time, I have come to know that God loves me. Yes, Jesus died for everyone, but what matters now is that I know He died for me.

Transitions in our lives never really come to an end. The kids are almost grown and changes in our lives seem to happen more rapidly. As I have grown in my understanding of God's love and grace, I have seen my wife grow as well. We have become not only a couple but a team. We often are serving God, side-by-side, following His lead. His grace is ever present. Jesus told each of us that He would never leave us or forsake us. If my story helps you see this in your own life, I am thankful. For myself, I know it is true. God is a gracious God who has always desired to bless me. He has given me a new life beyond the abuse, a life which is fuller and richer than I could have ever dreamed. Now that I have come to know God really does love me and want me, I have become more attune to seeing His presence and work in not only my life but the lives of those around me. The Scriptures are still and will always be my foundation of truth, but with that said, I listen. There are many times when there is a prompting in my heart or a word from my wife which will send me off in a totally different direction than I was previously heading. In those times God teaches me something new or opens the way for service in a way I did not expect. His grace is still going before and opening the way. This will be the way it is for the rest of my earthly life. The way it is supposed to be! God is present in the lives of His people until His people are present with Him to share His life for all eternity.

As I close our time together, I want you to understand something which is vital to my life. I have not arrived! I am not fully beyond the hurt of the abuse I suffered. There are moments when I have an overwhelming sense of despair and failure. Thankfully, I have a wife who can sense those times in my life and who is ready to speak the truth to me. The feelings of worthlessness which come from time to time are a lie! While it is important to see God's presence and working in the past, it is also vital that we understand His working in our lives today. When God looks at you and I what does He see? At various points in my life I would have had many different answers, none of them good. My answer in those moments of darkness would not have revealed what God saw in me but what I saw and believed about myself. The hurts and pain of our childhood do color our perception of our own value. We convince ourselves we have no value. We are worthless. God has never and He will never believe this about you or me or any other person in this world. Each of us was created by God as a unique individual with a unique purpose. We were created to experience God—His love, His grace, even His forgiveness in a unique way. Because each of us in different, Jesus had to suffer uniquely for

Each of us was created by God as a unique individual with a unique purpose.

each one of us on the cross. He did this for me, and He did this for you precisely because God wants you. His heart, God's heart, is filled with joy and expectation for you. He is working to accomplish healing and give you hope. He is opening the way before you by His grace so He can reveal Himself to you in a greater way. Then, if you are willing, God will use you to touch the hearts of others and you will see Him accomplish the impossible.

Life is truly a journey. There are the mountain tops and together, you and I, we know there are the deep dark valleys, but we never journey alone. God is faithful! He will see us through each valley and over each mountain top until our journey is completed. Then, because God really does love us, the real journey of life will begin.

> *Praise be to the God and Father of our Lord Jesus Christ, the Father of compassion and the God of all comfort, who comforts us in all our troubles, so that we can comfort those in any trouble with the comfort we ourselves receive from God.* **2 Corinthians 1:3-4**

I end where I began, with the lyrics of a song which is sung by Matthew West. While Christian music in general us uplifting, this particular song resonated with me as I concluded my writing. God's heart is for His children and in the end, Grace Wins!

"Grace Wins"

by Matthew West

In my weakest moment I see you
Shaking your head in disgrace
I can read the disappointment
Written all over your face
Here comes those whispers in my ear
Saying who do you think you are
Looks like you're on your own from here
Cause grace could never reach that far

But, in the shadow of that shame
Beat down by all the blame
I hear you call my name sayin it's not over
And my heart starts to beat
So loud now, drowning out the doubt
I'm down but I'm not out

There's a war between guilt and grace
And they're fighting for a sacred space
But I'm living proof
Grace wins every time

No more lying down in death's defeat
Now I'm rising up in victory
Singing hallelujah
Grace wins every time

Words can't describe the way it feels
When mercy floods a thirsty soul
A broken side begins to heal
And grace returns what guilt has stole

And, in the shadow of that shame
Beat down by all the blame
I hear you call my name sayin it's not over
And my heart starts to beat
So loud now, drowning out the doubt
I'm down but I'm not out

There's a war between guilt and grace
And they're fighting for a sacred space
But I'm living proof
Grace wins every time

No more lying down in death's defeat
Now I'm rising up in victory
Singing hallelujah
Grace wins every time
For the prodigal son, grace wins
For the woman at the well, grace wins
For the blind man and the beggar, grace wins
For always and forever, grace wins

For the lost out on the street, grace wins
For the worst part of you and me, grace wins
For the thief on the cross, grace wins
For a world that it lost

There's a war between guilt and grace
And they're fighting for a sacred space
But I'm living proof
Grace wins every time

No more lying down in death's defeat
Now I'm rising up in victory
Singing hallelujah
Grace wins every time

Every time
I'm living proof grace wins every time